Blueprints for Success

Blueprints
for
Success

Joel Black
JJ Childers
Wade Cook
Keven Hart
Debbie Losse
Tim Semingson
Rich Simmons
Dan Wagner
Dave Wagner
Steve Wirrick
Gregory Witt

Lighthouse Publishing Group, Inc.
Seattle, Washington

Copyright © 1998 Wade Cook Seminars, Inc.

ISBN: 0-910019-60-6
Library of Congress Cataloging-in-Publication Data in process

"This publication is designed to provide accurate and authoritative information in regard to the subject matter covered. It is sold with the understanding that the publisher is not engaged in rendering legal, accounting,
or other professional service. If legal or other expert assistance is required,
the services of a competent professional person should be sought." From a
declaration of principles jointly adopted by a committee of the American
Bar Association and the committee of the Publisher's Association.

Balance of Power™ and MoneyStream™ are the exclusive intellectual property of Worden Brothers, Inc. The descriptions and analysis of these indicators have been used with their permission. For further information contact
Worden Brothers, Inc., 5 Oaks Office Park, 4905 Pine Cone Drive, Durham,
North Carolina 27707, 1-800-776-4940.

Book Design by Judy Burkhalter
Dust Jacket by Cynthia Fliege

Published by Lighthouse Publishing Group, Inc.
14675 Interurban Avenue South
Seattle, WA 98168-4664
1-800-706-8657
206-901-3100 (fax)

Printed in the United States of America
First Edition
10 9 8 7 6 5 4 3 2 1

To the spouses and friends of small business owners, entrepreneurs, and investors, who put up with so much.

This book would not be what it is without the help of Cherlye Hamilton, Jerald Miller, Alison Curtis, Mark Engelbrecht, Angela Wilson, Connie Suehiro, Brent Magarrell, Judy Burkhalter, Bethany McVannel and Cynthia Fliege. We sincerely appreciate the hard work each of these people have put into this book.

Contents

Preface

uccess comes in many forms. Some people say that if you own a big house, have a lot of money, a swimming pool, a glamorous wife or handsome husband, and the finest, hottest car on the block, you are successful. However, success doesn't always come in the form of material possessions or people who make you look better.

We are of the opinion that if you have a great attitude, satisfying relationships with those whom you live and work with, and worship God, you have success in your life. These are some of the basic blueprints of life.

Adding to this set of blueprints can add to your successful life. The chapters in this book were written by successful speakers of Wade Cook Seminars, Inc. They each believe that the philosophies they work and live by will help you in plotting your blueprints whether you are at the beginnings of a successful life or prepared to retire.

Wade Cook, who wrote the chapter "How Ya Gonna Succeed, Jack?" retired (the first time) at the age of 29 after driving a cab, attending college, and making a living by making a profit from selling the houses he purchased. Eventually, this became known as the real estate cash flow system, and his ensuing book, *Real Estate Money Machine,* was the result.

Debbie Losse's chapter on Covered Calls And Success covers the gamut from fear of the stock market to calculating yields and how to make a sizeable profit writing covered calls. You'll enjoy reading Debbie's writing style as she explains the covered call strategy.

JJ Childers writes that you can solve some of your financial problems by focusing on three critical areas: asset protection, estate planning, and tax reduction. He discusses each one of these areas one by one in his chapter "Planning For Success." He has learned from his father and others around him that it is important to plan ahead for your future and implement the strategies you believe in.

We believe you will read these strategies of life and the stock market with renewed and enhanced vision. You may learn more from one author/speaker or another and find that the blueprints in your own life will have some editions and additions. Blueprints tend to go through several revisions before the final one is approved. So, be ready for positive changes in your philosophies while you read this, and let us know how it changes your life!

Successful Thinking

Dan Wagner

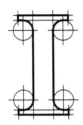have had the opportunity while traveling across the country to meet and get to know many people. What a wonderful experience. Many of them are successful businessmen and women. One of my favorite questions to ask is: in your opinion what is the biggest difference between success and failure? As you can imagine, I receive some very interesting remarks. Some people say college degrees, working hard, never giving up, follow through, the way you dress, enthusiasm, and being at the right place at the right time. While all these things help in becoming successful I believe that there is one ingredient that most people overlook. I have also found that very successful people all have this one thing in common. *They are in control of what they think!*

> You can make more friends in two months by becoming interested in other people than you can in two years by trying to get people interested in you.
>
> *Dale Carnegie*

Some of you are thinking: "This guy is crazy!" I'm in control of my thoughts, and I'm not wealthy. My answer to that is: control over your thoughts in the wealth-building process doesn't happen overnight. It is a pattern that has to be developed over a period of months or even years. We have all heard the adage, "As a man thinketh, so

1

shall he become," which indicates to me that it does not happen all at once. It has been shown in many different studies that criminals don't decide in a day to go out and rob a bank. When interviewed, they all have said it happened because they were caught up in the thought process for a very long time, that the excitement mounted the longer they pondered. In most cases they said their thoughts simply took over. So what is the key to success or failure? We become what we think about! Throughout history, prophets, wise men, and philosophers disagreed on many things but on this one great truth they all agreed. Ralph Waldo Emerson said, "A man is what he thinks about all day long." William James said, "The greatest discovery of my generation is that human beings can alter their lives by altering their attitudes of mind." He also said, "We need only act as if the thing in question were real and it will become infallibly real by growing in such a connection with our lives that it will become real. It will become so knit with habit and emotion that our interest in it will be those which characterize belief." He also said, "If you only care enough for a result you will almost certainly obtain it. If you wish to be learned, you will be learned. If you wish to be rich, you will be rich. If you wish to be good, you will be good." But you truly must wish for them.

> **A man is what he thinks about all day long.**
>
> *Ralph Waldo Emerson*

Time out here—be very careful what you wish for. I'm reminded of a commercial I recently saw on television. A genie appeared to a young man and granted him three wishes. The young man was very excited. His first wish was to have all the money in the world. Boom! There it was, all in a heap. His second wish was to have a large harem of beautiful women, and it was granted. The genie said, "You have one more wish."

The young man, thinking very hard, said, "Okay, I wish for everlasting life." Immediately the Genie turned him into the Eveready Bunny! He got his wish, but because of it, he lost his first two. Be very careful what you wish for. It can come to pass.

This has been a great discovery for me and I only wish I had learned it years earlier. The law simply stated is:

If you think in negative terms you will get negative results. If you think in positive terms, you achieve positive results.

Like the law of gravity, it is unbendable. If you jump off a building, you will go down 100% of the time. What you tell your mind it will give back 100% of the time. This is the basis of the *law* of prosperity and success. You have to believe in order to succeed.

So how does this work? Why do we become what we think about? Let me tell you how it works. Here's an example: suppose a farmer has a good fertile field. The farmer has a choice: he may plant in the field whatever he chooses. The field doesn't care. The farmer has to make the decision.

Remember that we are comparing the field with the human mind. It doesn't care what you plant in it. It will return what you plant, but it doesn't care what you plant. For instance, the farmer has two seeds in his hand. One is wheat and the other is a seed of a poisonous plant. He digs two holes in the dirt and plants each of them. The field produces what is planted: one wheat and one poison.

> Speech is a mirror of the soul; as a man speaks, so he is.
>
> *Publilius Syrus*

The Bible tells us, "Whatsoever you sow, so shall you reap." Our minds are much like that field. It doesn't care what we plant, success or failure, a worthwhile goal or confusion, misunderstanding, or fear.

It doesn't matter what we plant; our minds contain riches beyond our wildest dreams. It will return whatever we plant.

Now you might say, "If that's true, why don't people use their minds more?" I think I may have an answer for that too. How many times have you been given something for free? What has happened to it ? How much importance did you place on it? You see, we were taught to believe that the things we get for free are of little value, and the things we pay money for are of great value. In reality, it's the things we receive free that are most meaningful to us—our bodies, our brains, our hopes and dreams, our families, our friends, our ambitions, and our love for country. All of these items are free, but the things that cost us money are very cheap and can be replaced at anytime. A good man can be completely devastated financially and later make another fortune. Our house can burn down and we can rebuild it. But the things we got for nothing we can never replace! The human mind isn't used because we take it for granted.

> You only live once, but if you work it right, once is enough.
>
> *Joe E. Lewis*

The mind can do anything it's assigned, but we usually give it little jobs to do instead of big jobs. University studies show the majority of people operate on 10% or less of their abilities. So now take the time to make the most important decision in your life. What is it you want?

Do you want to be the top sales person in your office?
Do you want to be a better worker?
Do you want to go places within your company?
Do you want to get RICH?

All you have to do is plant that seed in your mind, care for it, work steadily towards your goal and it will become a reality. Not only will it, it has to. You see, it's a law.

As I mentioned previously, picture yourself having already achieved this goal. See yourself doing the things that you will be doing when you reach your goal. All the pressures and stress we feel in our lives are caused by our own thoughts. You are where you are because it's really where you want to be—whether you will admit it or not. What you think next week, next month, and next year, will determine your future and mold your life. You're guided by your mind.

Think for a moment about your car. All by itself the car is beautiful, but it can't go anywhere. It can fill no real purpose. But you get in, turn it on, and you can direct it anywhere you would like to go. Would you drive it into a ditch and leave it there? Or would you do your best to keep it on the road, headed in the direction previously determined? The answer, I hope, is obvious, but this is exactly how the brain works. Unless you get in and turn it on you will constantly be in a state of confusion, uncertainty, fear, and doubt.

You need to take charge of your thoughts. Give your mind some direction and once it's pointing in the right direction, continue to plant the things that will help you achieve the things you're after.

Goethe said, "I respect the man who knows distinctly what he wishes. The greater part of all the mischief in the world arises from the fact that men do not sufficiently understand their own aims."

> **Without some goal and some efforts to reach it, no man can live.**
>
> *Fydor Dostoevsky*

Now that I have explained the process, we need to put it to the test. For the next 90 days I want you to test the theory. It won't be easy, but neither is the road to success. The path to wealth is a bumpy road. Fortunately, there are many who have traveled the path before us, smoothing and moving some of the larger obstacles out of the way. Remember, you cannot achieve anything great without paying a price. The results of your 90 day experiment will be in direct proportion to the effort you put forth. To be a lawyer or doctor you must pay the price of long years of difficult study. To be successful in selling we must be willing to pay the price.

What is the price? First, we must understand that we literally become what we think about. We must control our thoughts. Remember "as ye sow, so shall ye reap." Second, cut away from the mind all distractions, allowing it to take off and soar as it was designed. Understand that your limitations are self imposed, that you have enormous opportunities in your life, and that it is all up to you to achieve them. It's rising above pettiness and narrow-minded prejudices. It's not loading your life with a bunch of negativism.

> **Genius is the ability to put into effect what is in your mind.**
>
> *F. Scott Fitzgerald*

I have found that many people dwell on their problems too much. When something doesn't go their way, they stew about it or hold grudges towards others. Remember, this type of thought pattern can only lead to failure. You must immediately replace these thoughts with uplifting and positive thoughts directed towards the outcome you desire. I have a favorite phrase which my family and close friends know me by. Whenever I hear someone complaining, I tell him," GET OVER IT!" Why worry about the things you have no control over? If you do have control over a particular problem, fix it, and then GET OVER IT.

The other night I was feeling disappointed and discouraged about the way the seminar I had given that afternoon had gone. I was not thinking clearly and was beating myself up for the way I presented the material. I knew that was the reason no product was sold. I decided to call my wife, Alice. As I moaned and bellyached, she graciously listened, then she said she loved me and hung up the phone. Still not satisfied, I continued complaining in my mind. I tried to get some rest. As I was dozing off, the phone rang. It was Alice again. She said, "Honey, I have been thinking about what you told me earlier, and I have an answer. GET OVER IT." Oh, how I hated to hear that. I had repeated that line so many times to others, but I knew she was right. She told me that I needed to take time to visualize my next seminar and the success that I was going to have, the people responding to my instructions and moving to the back table to purchase the products. I thanked her, told her I loved her and hung up the phone. From that moment on I felt a change in my heart and in my mind. The next day, after following her instructions, the seminar turned out to be a huge success.

> You can't have a better tomorrow if you are thinking about yesterday all the time.
>
> *Charles F. Kettering*

Third, allow your mind to think positive thoughts, to set a definite and clearly defined goal for yourself, and let your mind think about your goal from all possible angles. Let your imagination think and live many different possible solutions, then refuse to believe that anything can stand in the way of accomplishing your purpose. Act promptly and know that you are standing in the middle of your own gold mine.

Fourth, save at least 15% of your profits. Before we go any further, let me explain one more bit of wisdom that I have learned. It comes from the scriptures. Many places in the Bible it talks about the mind and the heart being one. If our heart (what we feel) is not in harmony with our mind, what we think generally will not be accomplished.

Let me give you a few examples to illustrate this point. Have you ever decided you wanted to lose weight? Your mind is fixed on your goal, however in your heart you really don't feel like exercising or cutting down on your food intake. Who wins? Your heart or your mind? Your heart does, 100% of the time.

Take an eight-year-old boy at an amusement park. Does he have to put a lot of effort into running from ride to ride? No, because his heart is into it. He is having fun. Is it hard for a person who loves to fish to get up at 4:00 AM or even earlier? No! Why? Because in his heart he would rather do nothing else. This is how it has to be with your goals. Not only must you think about them, you also have to feel them enough to act on them.

> **The successful people are the ones who can think up stuff for the rest of the world to keep busy at.**
>
> *Don Marquis*

Fifth: action. Without action ideas are worthless! What would have happened if Alexander Graham Bell had never acted on his idea for the telephone? Or the Wright brothers never attempted to put their idea in the air? How many ideas have been shelved or even scrapped because you were afraid to act on them? In order to succeed you have got to take action.

Let's review quickly the five points discussed here:

1. You will become what you think about.
2. Imagination: let your mind soar and ponder.
3. Courage: concentrate on your goal every day.
4. Save 15% of what you earn.
5. Action: without it, ideas are worthless.

Now let's talk about the 90-day test:

1. Write on a card what it is you want more than anything else. Perhaps it's more money or a new home. Perhaps you would like to double your income. Write it specifically and write only one thing. Define it clearly. Carry it with you so you can look at it several times a day. Then start thinking about it, at work, before bed, early in the morning so that you have something to look forward to, a reason to get out of bed. Remember, the item is yours the minute you start thinking about it and write it down.

2. Here's the hard part: stop thinking about what you fear. Whenever a negative thought or picture comes into your mind, replace it with a mental picture of your positive and worthwhile goal. There will be times when you feel like giving up. Human nature is to dwell on the negative because it is easier, and this is why only 5% of the people are successful. You must begin right now to place yourself in the "5% group" who become successful. You must take control of your mind for the next 90 days. Your mind will only think about what you allow it to think.

For the next 90 days give of yourself more than you have ever given before, do more than you have to do, and go the extra mile. What you get in this life is in direct proportion to what you give. However, if you give to get, then you're not really giving anything, you're trading. You need to learn to give, whether you get anything in return or not. I have found myself many times in my life giving of my time and talents to help others, expecting nothing in return. The satisfaction that I was able to help was enough for me. However, the more I gave, the more I received.

> There are not traffic jams when you go the extra mile.
>
> *Anonymous*

As you focus for the next 90 days on your goals, things will happen in your life that, before, were nothing but mere wishes. Take the test. Try it. You will be amazed at the difference in your life.

I hope that all of the things mentioned in this chapter have helped you to frame and focus your thoughts so that you can put each of them into action. Instinctively, you already knew many of them. Now you must prove them for yourself. So many things in our lives seem to be at war with these laws. However, if you take them, put them to the test and practice them in your life, you will be moving ahead and growing. Those who don't will never move, but will flounder aimlessly, never able to reach success. So learn them and use them well and success will be yours!

Success is that old ABC—ability, breaks, and courage.

Charles Luckman

About The Author

an Wagner is the embodiment of personal, family, interpersonal, and professional success. No one is more fun to be around or more insightful in a discussion. After rising to the top in the delivery industry, Dan was looking for a chance to earn more, be of more value to his community, and especially to spend more time with his family. He found it in investing and teaching others how to invest successfully. He immediately used the success strategies he had learned over the years, his work ethic, and his high energy to amass a sizable personal fortune, and to teach others how to do the same.

Now he is producing movies, consulting nationally, training other consultants, and spending more quality time with his son and four daughters. He is CEO and President of two corporations, and is often called upon to clarify business issues.

Dan is most excited about *The Creator's Game*, the first full-length movie ever filmed on LaCrosse, which is currently in production. It is due to be released in 1998.

Dan has been married 16 years to his lovely wife Alice and they are expecting a sixth child in May.

Successful Ways

Joel Black

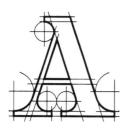As I began my 13 year university experience, I ended up learning a tremendous amount in an immense number of areas. I discovered I had some aptitude and talent in several areas, perhaps not the leader of the field, but enough so that I could find work. I was offered jobs in two or three different areas and eventually found myself teaching school.

I did not get into teaching school until I was over 30. I had a wealth of experiences up until that time, and so, I ended up being a pretty doggone good school teacher. All in all, it was an excellent experience, a good job, and it was fun! I know that not everybody can say that they enjoy their work, but I did enjoy mine. There were elements of it I did not enjoy, such as the paperwork and the parent conferences. Yet, for the most part I did enjoy my job. Some of the elements I really enjoyed were the perks. In teaching, of course, the perks are June, July and August.

> Don't try to fix the students, fix ourselves first. The good teacher makes the poor student good and the good student superior. When our students fail, we, as teachers, too, have failed.
>
> *Marva Collins*

I was taking advantage of that time in the summer to go up in the mountains. I love the mountains, hiking, and doing outdoor things.

I would take groups of young people—students, and go up there and teach them how to hike and rappel off cliffs. They learned how to identify plants, animals, and rocks, and we would have a good time. So, all things told, this was a good job. It was supporting me.

My family and I were getting by in a small house with a leaky roof where we had placed some plastic under the eaves to drain the water toward the outside. The kids were all piled together in two bedrooms. We were doing reasonably well. We were a happy family having a good time. There was a lot of love in our home, a lot of peace, and a lot of singing. In the front yard we had flowers, beautiful flowers. People would always stop in the front of our home to stare and point, and talk to us about the yard. So, all things looked really good.

> Anything you're good at contributes to happiness.
>
> *Bertrand Russell*

Though I loved my position, I had to admit that there really wasn't much at the end of the road. I would be teaching until I was 65, 70, or 75, and then I would probably retire. Social Security would probably be bankrupt, and my teacher's pension would give me about half of what I was used to living on at that point in time. But, the children would be out of the home. I really wouldn't need life insurance at that point. The house would be paid for, so I could probably live on half. That was the world I was facing, and I would work until I was very old. Then I would go home and spend ten or twelve years reading the books that I'd always meant to read, and watching the videos that I'd always meant to watch. Eventually, that would be the end of life in this domain and I would move on to the next world. I had great faith and hope in the next life, the life after death.

I met a gentleman who came up with one of the groups of young people in the summer of '93. I was running a program for young people up in the mountains. He began to talk to me about his life as a financial wizard.

This gentleman had made a fortune in real estate, he had run a printing company, and an advertising company as well. He had been in three or four different businesses, all of them successful. He was getting involved in the stock market, and he was being successful there. It seemed like he had a talent for money. Anything he touched, it seemed, would turn to gold. It was his hobby. Now my hobby was reading books, and I was very good at reading, I could read fast. And his hobby was money, and it seemed like anything he did worked. He had the ability to generate cash out of thin air. He could simply dream something, and then go make it happen.

> The first step towards success in any occupation is to become interested in it.
>
> *Sir William Osler*

This was a whole new concept to me, because my sense had always been: well, I can have dreams, but how do you make them happen? He would simply have an idea, generate energy around him, and make things happen. For instance, he recently wrote a book called *Don't Set Goals*. I said to myself, "How is it that he could distill all my best thinking and experience into such a useful and readable book when he and I have never discussed this topic?" Clearly his life and experience have taught him the same lessons I have learned. It was incredible to meet this guy, and have him tell me his story. He told me how he was making $10,000 a day, and by coming out on the wilderness program with us he was giving up $10,000 a day to be there. I was very, very intrigued.

Being interested in knowledge, I asked if it would be possible to sit down with him again, and talk more, and pick his brain. He invited me to come to a seminar, and learn some highlights of his life and career, come to understand who he was, and come to understand some things that I did not understand about free enterprise, about America, about capitalism, and about generating wealth. I was very pleased to attend that workshop, and learn from him—have my eyes opened. Suddenly, for the first time in my life, I got my mind around an idea, the idea that it might be possible for me, a school teacher, a fellow who had somewhat reached the end of the line, to reach those dreams of travel and cultures, altruism and service. Those goals were ones that I had only dreamed of, and they weren't really goals yet; they were hopes. But I was able to get my mind wrapped around the idea that they might be possible if I could just learn what this guy knew.

> I not only use all the brains I have, but all I can borrow.
>
> *Woodrow Wilson*

He taught me about success as a mental construct. Success has very little to do with outward appearance, very little to do with money and the kinds of things you can put your hands on. It begins in the mind. It begins in a belief, and not just a belief, but that is where it begins. The belief, then, makes you believe certain things, disbelieve others, love certain things, and not love others. Belief makes you go towards certain things, and away from others, accept some things, and reject others. This belief system is a foundation that predisposes you to take advantage of opportunities, to be successful, and be ready to roll.

So, he said, "Put it in your mind, these ideas, these things that you want to accomplish. These things that you've told me about are possible. The American dream is alive and well. Horatio Alger stories continue to occur. People arrive as immigrants, and people are born in poverty. People with the least likely scenario for success become successful every day in America, every day."

I spent some time trying to wrap my mind around the sense of, "What would I be like to be rich? What would it be like to have the money to travel, to go places, to retire before I got to the age of 75? What would that be like?" I tried to envision and use mental rehearsal. Steven Covey, author of *Seven Habits of Highly Effective People*, talks about this tremendous power that can come from mental rehearsal.

> If you want to give me a present, give me a good life. That's something I can value.
>
> *Raymond Massey*

This is what I did, and it paid off. I would get these incredibly detailed pictures in my mind of me in these settings and with these opportunities.

It was then I discovered another key to success: we become what we think about all day long. We move toward those things that are in our minds. Having planted these vivid images in my mind, I couldn't help but think about them. Because they were so attractive and so appealing to me, and they fit so well with the things I wanted, so vivid and detailed, I couldn't help but move towards those things that I thought about all day long.

Suddenly, I found myself being offered the opportunity to go to work for this gentleman and help him design programs. I could get on the cutting edge of wealth generation and learn the principles of financial freedom. I was reading books and listening to tapes. With this opportunity, I then had a tremendous dilemma. I was caught between taking a risk, and staying with the secure position I was in. I had tenure, esteem, and a regular paycheck. It wasn't much, but I knew how much it was, and I learned to live on it. I had that security which couldn't be taken from me, because there will always be a need for teachers. I could leave it all behind without security, a guaranteed income, and without knowing what the future would hold. But it would be with a person who knew how to make money, and maybe I could learn from him how to make money, too. Maybe he could help me find my dreams. My dream originally had been to run wilderness programs and travel/study programs for students; that is what I really love.

Here was a possibility of learning how to make that happen. So, do I take the risk or stay with my secure position? Do I jump into the unknown? That was a difficult decision. Oh, how that tore at me. I was so afraid, constantly afraid. So, naturally, I went to family, friends and colleagues for advice, and every one of them said, "Don't jump. You've got security and predictability. You know where you are. Don't jump." Yet, it gnawed at my insides. "Should I leave something I love, and go into something that I don't know anything about?" Well, I knew a little about it, but not a lot. What I knew held a promise, and I had to make that decision. Oh, that was tough. I finally made the decision to leave teaching. I went to the principal and said, "I'm gonna take a leave of absence. I may jump, I may never come back, I don't know." Permission was given for me to take the leave of absence, and to make that jump into a whole new life.

> **A person who walks in another's tracks leaves no footprints.**
>
> *Anonymous*

The biggest barrier to success, for 99% of the people in this country is that courage to step beyond the light into the darkness, and jump into the unknown. The fear of the unknown is the strongest fear there is. We're not afraid of a plane crash and death so much as we're afraid of what's beyond death. We're not afraid of the pain of cancer so much as we're afraid of what it's going to be like to be there.

I talk to people all the time who have been through horrible accidents, devastating losses, terrible diseases, and they said, "You know, once I was in the middle of it, I could deal with it. Once I was in the middle of the pain, I could deal with it. Once I was in the middle of the tragedy, I could deal with it. It was the fear before the fact, the fear of the unknown, that was so debilitating." That's the way it is with all of us.

The next principle of success that I learned was to stare down the fear, march right up the center of it and out the back end. That's what one has to do. There's just no secret way to do it.

This brings up the next key to success: knowledge, specific knowledge. I had a ton of knowledge and knew so much about so many areas that people sometimes called me an encyclopedia. However, I did not have the specific knowledge that would put money in my account. This is the specific knowledge that I began to learn from Wade Cook, the gentleman I met in the mountains that summer.

Of course, from my own background I knew that once you had knowledge, you had to apply it. And so, I began applying the principles that I learned. As I gained specific knowledge about investment or real estate, I began to apply those principles. I formed my own corporation, reduced my taxes, and learned to think as a CEO. I began to do things in a way that America is designed around, as a small, private corporation. I began to reap the rewards immediately in terms of reduced taxes and greater opportunities.

> **Wisdom is the power to put our time and our knowledge to the proper use.**
>
> *Thomas J. Watson*

Good heavens, this was amazing! That was the power of compound returns, of course. But the amazing thing was that I could do it.

I had the specific knowledge that allowed me to examine the market and other investment opportunities It allowed me to make decisions that were 85 or 90% accurate and manage my own money in such a way that it grew. Now, of course, I diversified, because every once in awhile I made a mistake. Everybody makes mistakes, and occasionally you pick something that goes south. I was doing phenomenally well. I had 150% on my investment, after just 13 months. I was so pleased.

That brings me to another principle of success: what goes around, comes around. I firmly believe I would have never met Wade Cook if I had not already been giving. I firmly believe that I would not have been able to learn so much, and manage my money so well, had I not already been giving things back. I believe that nature and God watch out for their own, and that those who give back receive more abundantly. In fact, that's an ancient Hebrew proverb, and I have found it to be true in my own life. It is a principle of success.

> The older we get, the more we realize that service to others is the only way to stay happy. If we do nothing to benefit others, we will do nothing to benefit ourselves.
>
> *Carl Holmes*

Another principle of success that I've lived all my life, and I didn't realize how powerful it is, is spend 10% of your income on furthering your opportunities. This includes furthering your education and acquiring more knowledge and more expertise. Now, I've done this all my life simply because of my hobby of diving into books. I've always been learning, and continue to see the payoff. Because of this, I was prepared when it was time to teach all of those extra classes, travel to Europe, write a book, cut a tape set, or give a speech. Due to this continual learning, I believe I was also prepared to make the jump over to work with Mr. Cook.

This is a powerful principle. Whatever money you earn, live on it. But not on all of it, only on 80% of it. Give 20% back—10% to charity and 10% to your own future and education. Investing in learning new principles, your careers, and tasks that will give you greater opportunities and a greater future. That's a vital part, and that's a lot of money. Now, if you want to retire rich, I suggest that you take another 10 to 15% and put it into investments. All of a sudden, you have to live on 65% of what you make.

That brings us to another principle of success: no excuses, just do it. There was a religious leader that I greatly admired, who had a little sign on his desk that was simply four letters long. Two words, it said, "Do it." I like that. Just get in there and do it. So you live on 65%, invest 15%, give 10% back, and put 10% into education. What a powerful situation. That 15% is compounding like crazy. Your education is allowing you to make more and more. Suddenly, the 65% of what you're making is more than the 100% of what you used to make before.

> **A journey of a thousand miles must begin with a single step.**
>
> *Chinese proverb*

I have been out of teaching now for two years, next month. I walked away from the classroom, and walked away with regrets, doubts, misgivings, and a lot of fear. Now, I make more in a week than I used to make in a month. I ran into one of my friends that I used to teach with, and he said, "Joel, when are you coming back?" And I said, "Dick, you know I'd love to come back, but right now, I can't afford it." And he said, "That good, huh?" And I said, "You don't even know how good."

The American dream is alive and well. Success is in your hands. Success is in my hands. All of us can do it. I was a school teacher with seven children, one income, and $500 in my savings account, which

I moved to my brokerage account. Starting with $500 in my brokerage account, now suddenly, I'm going to be retired, five years after I started, as a multimillionaire. My income has already quadrupled from what I was as a teacher. What happened in there? What was different? What was different was that I got a firm picture in my mind, sucked in my stomach, doubled up my fist, marched to the edge of the light, and took a step into the darkness. I'm succeeding by learning, risking, doing, and taking control—there it is.

> **Who dares to teach must never cease to learn.**
>
> *John Cotton Dana*

About The Author

oel Black is a nationally recognized educator garnering a variety of awards. He is also a pioneer in the home-schooling and experiential education fields. In 1994, he incorporated his small education business, founded his own high school and began learning how to invest successfully in the stock market. By 1997 he was out of debt and financially independent.

Joel is the author of two books: *While You Wait* and *What Everyone Needs to Know About Experiential Education*. He has also authored many articles on education, business, investment, leadership, and recreation issues. He has spoken in all 50 states at education conventions and investment workshops. Recently, he has created a public school home-school liaison program in his home state and an investment workshop for high school youth.

Joel lists as his greatest accomplishments, his many former students who have gone on to national prominence and his family: eight children and a wife who love him, even through all the years.

Joel is a rappel instructor, a risk taker, a problem solver, and a man who loves variety. "God has been gracious to us," he says. "Life is wonderful."

Successful Timing

Dave Wagner

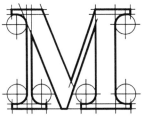ost people who have had major success would concede that they were in the right place at the right time. So, how do they continually have such great success? How are they able to regularly be in the right place at the right time?

First of all, they do not sit in one place and just wait for it to be the right place. They are continually moving, looking for the right place. You can not find the right place if you are not looking for it.

> **Make every decision as if you owned the whole company.**
>
> *Robert Townsend*

That reminds me of the of the man who, before he went to bed, prayed, "Dear Lord, please let me win the lottery." Every night he would repeat this prayer. This went on for quite some time and then one night he asked the Lord, "I have been praying to win the lottery for a long time now. Why don't you ever answer my prayers?"

Then he heard a voice from heaven, and it said, "You have to at least meet me halfway and buy a ticket." You cannot win the lottery if you don't buy a ticket.

I am not saying that we should run out and buy lottery tickets. What I am saying is that so many individuals are looking for success, yet they are not willing to do what is required to get it.

Once you have learned the strategies and techniques to be successful in the options market (that is buying and selling options on stock split companies) the question always arises, "Well, when do I purchase the options, before or after the stock split?"

The answer, of course, is up to you, but I have found that you can be very successful at either time.

> Gossip is when you hear something you like about someone you don't.
>
> *Earl Wilson*

Where do rumors come from? I don't know how the word gets out, probably by some secretary or inner-office memo overseen by the janitor or security guard. Once the word gets out though, it doesn't take too long to spread, especially if it means that someone can make money from the deal.

I received my information through some of my associates. I am not sure where they got it. I just know that whenever I hear a rumor, I check it out completely before I act on it.

I recommend that you always do your homework. Surround yourself with information. Educate yourself. Do not rely on one source only. Pull up the charts and see what their history looks like. Ask your broker about the history of the company. Ask about their profits and earnings. Delve in and find out all you can.

Note: it is truly a wise individual who can learn from the experience of others. If you know of someone who is successful in the market and consistently is getting the kinds of monthly returns that you are seeking, then why wouldn't you follow his lead?

If you were standing before a mine field and you looked across it and saw someone waving to you to cross I believe that anyone but a fool would follow in the footsteps of the individual who successfully made it across with both legs intact. You would carefully place your foot inside of his print in the sand, and would be sure not to waver from his steps one bit. The stock market is a mine field. (It, too, can dismember you financially.) If you want to be able to get to the other side in one piece, you should follow the footsteps of someone who has been to the other side. Follow the proven strategies and techniques that will get you to the other side in one piece.

The stock market, like any other market, is driven by supply and demand. If the owners of the stock sell their shares to capture their profits, then naturally there is a larger surplus of stock, thereby reducing the price of said stock.

Note: never put all of your money on one play. Diversify your plays. That way, if one of the stocks goes down, it doesn't affect everything you are doing, only that portion that is in that particular stock. Although we have learned how to minimize our risk, there are still very real risks inherent in the stock market.

Education and location

Look to be in the right place at the right time. Many of us have been there and didn't even know it until the time had passed us by. If you want to recognize the right place and time when it is upon you, you have to know what you are looking for, and education is the key. Become enlightened.

> Power is not revealed by striking hard or often, but by striking true.
>
> *Honore' de Balzac*

Education is power. Education is control. You should seek first to educate yourself in financial matters. If you are to take charge and be in control, read everything you can get your hands on. Subscribe to every magazine that will give you insight to financial matters. Study the IRS codes, attend seminars, and do whatever it takes to surround yourself with knowledge.

To learn how to swim you cannot just sit on the side of the pool and splash yourself. You have to get into the water. You have to surround yourself with the substance you wish to master which will buoy you up and allow you to get to the other side of the pool. What you were initially afraid of (the water) soon becomes your friend and allows you to overcome your fears. Education too, though some are afraid of it, will give you that same sense of freedom and accomplishment. If you are to be involved in the stock market, you need to recognize the risks and learn to avoid as much loss as possible.

The next question that I would like to address is: "Where do you recommend that someone, who is new at this, start?"

I suggest that you start with education; surround yourself with information. Study what the wealthy do. Listen to those who are where you want to be. Read everything that you can get your hands on.

Some people think that education is expensive and if you are one of those, then I say, "Continue on in ignorance and it will take you right back to where you have been." You only pay for education once and then it is all yours. No one can take that away from you. Fill your head with knowledge. Surround yourself with experience. Watch what the wealthy do and do it. I would venture to say that what the wealthy do that no one else does is that they just do it! Find your course and follow it. Stop messing around. Either do what you have always done and be happy, or find a new path and get on with it.

> In the business world, everyone is paid in two coins: cash and experience. Take the experience first; the cash will come later.
>
> *Harold S. Geneen*

Education is a never-ending process. If you ever stop learning you have stopped all progression in life. We have all heard that old saying, "You cannot teach an old dog new tricks." That may be true, but we are not dogs, and we can always learn.

I was speaking to a gentleman at one of my seminars. He was sharp as a tack and he told me he was 90 years old. I asked him how he stayed so alert. He told me that the mind is just like the body. If you don't exercise it, it will deteriorate. It will shrivel up and die. I am no expert on these matters, but I believe that what he said is true. So exercise your mind. Fill it with knowledge. Keep learning. Don't let your mind shrivel up and die.

Join the computer age

The last question that I would like to address that always comes up is, "Do I need a computer to be involved in the stock market?" as if to say, "Is there any other way to get information?"

I have a degree in mechanical engineering and I was a computer system administrator for a while. As I travel around the country, I am amazed that so many people are afraid of computers. The answer to the

> Man is still the most extraordinary computer of all.
>
> *John F. Kennedy*

question, although qualified, is "yes." There are other ways to get information and you do not need a computer to invest in the stock market. However, you must understand that the computer age has brought with it an abundance of information.

From my computer at home, I can find out minute by minute stock quotes. I can pull up charts on companies that I am interested in, and I can find out the latest news on those companies. I can trade stocks and options 24 hours a day, seven days a week. Although the market is closed, my on-line broker can take my order and it will be traded on the next business day. So, although you do not need a computer to trade on the market, it is a tool that I have found to be invaluable.

If you decide that you want to have access to as much information as possible, so that your homework is complete and you can minimize your risk, I recommend that you consider getting a computer. By not having a computer you do not have instant access to charts, stock quotes, company histories and you will miss out on the opportunity of having WIN (Wealth Information Network) and being able to look over the shoulder of Wade Cook and his handpicked crew of stock market professionals (Team Wall Street).

Fulfill your desires

The road to wealth is not easy. In fact, my friend, Wade Cook, put it best in his new book, *Wall Street Money Machine* when he said, "The road to wealth is not a freeway. As a matter of fact, many times it is a very rocky road with many bumps, dips and detours along the way. Not only are most people not willing to take the risk, but many are not willing to get on the road."

> Don't try to die rich but live rich.
>
> *Thomas Bird Mosher*

As I mentioned before, I feel that by far the best investment is education. The Wall Street Workshop is the place to start. Get there. Learn what you need to do. Then use that knowledge to help you create wealth.

How bad do you want to be wealthy? What are you willing to sacrifice to get there?

I remember a younger gentleman who came to our seminar. When he went home and told his wife he wanted to go to the Wall Street Workshop she said, "No way." They didn't have the money. He wanted it so badly that he sold his motorcycle to pay for it.

You can always find a way to success if you are willing to sacrifice for it.

How many of you have said, "I would give anything to be rich." How many of you have said, "I would give anything to be able to spend more time with my family." Or, "I would give anything to have a new car, truck or boat."

Well, now is your time to prove it. It won't be easy, but you have the chance in front of you right now. Either take it or be satisfied with where you are.

Finally, it takes money to make money. That is the cold, hard truth. Not a lot of money, but it does take money. At the Wall Street Workshop you will find out how to take what money you have and make it work for you to maximize your returns. Come to the Wall Street Workshop. Learn the strategies that have made many of its graduates wealthy and prepare to make money. Prepare to turn your life around.

> The best career advice given to the young is, "Find out what you like doing best and get someone to pay you for doing it."
>
> *Katharine Whitehorn*

Don't let the next five years be the same as the last five years!

About The Author

ave Wagner is the oldest of fourteen children and has a bachelors degree in Mechanical Engineering. It was while acting as a computer systems administrator that he was given Wade's book, *Real Estate Money Machine*, and began putting it to the test. After much success in the real estate market, he sought out Wade Cook and his stock market strategies.

Dave has served Wade Cook as a speaker, and is now acting as a sales management executive for Wade Cook Seminars. He is the President and CEO of his own corporation specializing in internet consulting and web page design, and is involved in a limited partnership devoted to stock market investment strategies.

Dave has three books in the process of publication and two others that he is currently working.

Dave and his wife, Becky, have been married for 19 years and are the proud parents of seven children: David III, Ryan, Cristina, Patricia, Tamarah, Jonathan, and Jacob.

A Strategy For Success

Steve Wirrick

ome of the questions I love to ask people at our seminars are: "What are you looking for when you invest? You have taken time out of your day to come and spend it with us. Why? What are you wanting out of this information?" What has been interesting to me is that overwhelmingly, the same three basic answers keep coming back.

So to get started, I'd love to share those with you because it will lay the foundation for everything we'll discuss in these special reports.

The number one reason why people invest, and I don't care whether it's in the stock market, real estate, a business, or a franchise, is for the CASH FLOW. Obviously, that comes as no surprise. People want more money. In fact, how many of you find that you always have way more month than you do money?

> The darkest hour of any man's life is when he sits down to plan how to get money without earning it.
>
> *Horace Greeley*

The second reason why people invest is for tax write offs. They are sick and tired of working four months out of the year for Uncle Sam before they see a dime. They want to keep more of their money right in their own home, businesses, communities and churches.

> **It is not the return on my investment that I am concerned about; it is the return of my investment.**
>
> *Will Rogers*

The final reason why people invest is for GROWTH—the appreciation of the asset, so they and their families can have something to retire on. They want to stop trading time for money.

Furthermore, people want all three of those things at the same time, and they also want to get started with very little money.

What I find interesting is that real estate is one of only two investments that I know of where you can do just that. Where you can get cash flow, tax write-offs and growth, get them all at the same time and get started with very little money. In fact, with real estate you can still get started with no money.

Well, that begs the question, besides real estate, what's the other investment? Do you have any guesses? Stocks? Bonds? Options? REITs?

Let's put the stock market to the test, because here we are talking about the stock market—it has to fit our formula, right? Well, let's put it to the test and see what happens.

Cash Flow

When we invest in the stock market, are we always generating cash flow? No we don't. Uh-oh, we already have a problem. Now, if you buy-sell, buy-sell, hopefully you are, but let me ask you a question. Do you own stocks? Do you receive dividends on a quarterly, semi-annually, or annualized basis? If you know, what is the yield of those dividends? Pretty low, isn't it?! The average yield of all publicly traded companies is about 3 to 5%. The yield on the Standard and Poor's 500 is at a historic low right now—1.7%. Now if you're looking to get rich at 1.7% a year, is it going to happen? It's like we're on a slow boat going nowhere. In fact, if I mix in a little inflation of about 3% per year, are we going forwards or backwards? We actually may be losing ground!

Tax Write offs

If you have tax write offs in the stock market, what's that saying? Ugh, we're losing money. Ouch! Do you hate losing money? We all do. You can make $8,000 in a week, lose $600 on another play and it ruins the whole week. Did we make money? Sure we did, but you don't like losing money. I don't like losing money. So, how about latching ourselves onto strategies, a plan, a system, a way that will prevent us and keep us from losing money? It is definitely easier said than done. In fact, my special reports deal with just that.

> If you are truly serious about preparing your child for the future, don't teach him to subtract—teach him to deduct.
>
> *Fran Lebowitz*

Growth

Do stocks always go up? No they don't. They have a tendency to go down.

As you can see, the stock market has a hard time delivering on any one of these items, let alone all three at the same time. So what does?

Well, here's my curve ball for you. The only other investment I know of besides real estate that gives us CASH FLOW, TAX WRITE OFFS AND GROWTH, gives it to us all at the same time, and where we can still get started with very little money, is simply by running and operating your own small business. My own small business? Yes, your own small business. Now, stick with me here because it's critical to your trading style and lays the foundation upon which it is based.

Cash Flow

I would say the number one reason why people go into business for themselves is because they want more cash flow. They are sick and tired of working for somebody else. They hate having a boss breathing down their necks. They want to get paid what they are really worth. They want to call the shots. Having your own business provides such an opportunity.

Tax Write offs

If you had your own small business, you get more tax deductions than an individual. In fact, has Congress done a pretty good job of wiping out deductions for investment purposes? Yes, they have. But, if we do something for business purposes, can we still write that off? Yes! Are there things right now that we spend money on as individuals that we can't write off; but that if your business would buy it, we could write it off? You bet! What are some of those things? Car, gas, insurance, and computers

> Collecting more taxes than is absolutely necessary is legalized robbery.
>
> *Calvin Coolidge*

to name a few. In fact, that's why I love the seminar business, because instead of taking vacations, we're going to start taking what kind of trips? Business trips! Man, I love it. Now if you run into the beach, pool, or Mickey Mouse on your way to the business seminar, can you write it off? Talk to your accountant and they can bring you up to speed on how to set that up properly. The point is: do more in the name of business. Many of us overpay, that's right, overpay our taxes because we don't take advantage of all the deductions available to us. We can't get to where we want to be—financially independent if we keep sharing 40% of what we make with someone else.

Growth

Hopefully you're building a business for the future. So what's my point? My point is this:

If we are looking for cash flow, tax write offs and growth in our investments, and we are getting the same cash flow, tax write offs and growth by running and operating our own small businesses, why don't we marry those two things together. We need to start treating our investments like a business! I don't want that to slip by you as just another cute statement. It is powerful! It is key to your success. Start treating your investments like a business and watch your cash flow sky-rocket. Why? Because right now we have a tendency to do the exact opposite. We don't treat our investments like a business.

> We need to start treating our investments like a business!

Let's take a look at a typical retail business so I can show you what I mean. A business makes money by buying wholesale and selling retail. They buy in order to sell. But what have we been taught to do in the stock market? We buy and hold. Now, don't get me wrong. I'm not saying that you should sell all of your investments. I'm not saying you can't build up a nice portfolio. But think in terms of running your business like that. Someone walks into your store and wants to purchase something. You look them straight in the eye and say, "I can't sell you anything. We buy and hold in this store. We hold our inventory." I'm being facetious, but my point is a valid one. There's no money made until something is sold. Now, don't get me wrong. I love buying assets, but for many of us that's for the birds right now. Why? Because you are buying and holding instead of buying and selling! Can you be asset rich, yet cash poor? You better believe it! That's where a lot of us are in life. We have a bunch of stuff that looks good on paper, but we can't pay the bills. In fact, what buys the assets in the first place? If you bought a stock at $10 and it's trading at $100 today, have you made any money? No. Now, don't get me wrong, it looks great on paper but the last time I checked you couldn't buy groceries on margin. You can't put stock certificates in the gas tank. Can you quit your job? No. We're asset rich and cash poor. It's the cash flow that enables you to quit your job. It's the cash flow that enables you to take a vacation. It's the cash flow that pays for the kid's piano lessons, not the assets.

Let's go one step further. How many of you work for someone else? How long would it be before your income stops if you don't go to work? Perhaps you have your own business? How long before your business goes out of business if you don't go in to your place of business, your shop, your warehouse?

Business is like riding a bicycle. Either you keep moving or you fall down.

American business saying

What I'm alluding to is an income producing asset. For many of us, we are it. If our asset doesn't go to work, when does our income stop? Immediately.

I have a proposition for you. How about making it our goal to replace ourselves as the income producing asset, so the income keeps coming in whether we go to work or not. You could be at the beach, by the pool, or fast asleep in bed, and the money doesn't stop. Interested?

That's our goal. The American Dream. Financial Independence. Doing what you want, when you want to do it. What does that mean to you? Time with the kids, no debt, taking a trip around the world, or fixing up the car? Whatever it means to you, that is your goal!

In order to get you there, I need you to change your mindset just a little bit. By doing so, you'll open the window to so many possibilities financially. It'll blow your mind!

I need you to scrape together whatever cash you can. I need you to dump it into an asset. But instead of stopping there, and holding onto it like we are used to doing, I need you to get back to CASH! As quickly as possible. And that is our mantra: CASH - ASSET - CASH—the quicker the better. If you can do it in three weeks, great! In one day, fantastic! Better yet, how about within the hour? What it comes down to is treating your investments like a business. We buy in order to sell. The quicker the better!

When you start thinking like that, you will be able to make unbelievable amounts of cash. How about turning $300 into $1,200? Or, making an extra $1,200 to $2,500 a month? How about earning $40,000 a month or more! It's all possible if you but take the time to learn how to do it. It's that simple!

> Do you know the only thing that gives me pleasure? It's to see my dividends coming in.
>
> *John D. Rockefeller*

When you consider the unbelievable amounts of money you can make and how quickly you can make it trading options, you may ask yourself, "Why aren't more people doing this? If this is so great, wonderful and true, why haven't my brokers told me about it?"

Those are great questions, but too easy for me to answer, so, let me throw it back at you. If this is so great, wonderful and true, why aren't more people doing it?

I get varied responses, but ultimately they revolve around three areas, or "walls" as I like to call them. I call them walls because there are barriers in our lives that prevent us from getting what we want. If you could identify what the wall or walls are that are holding you back, would that have value? Yes! See, when we know what the walls are that are holding us back, we can then destroy them. What are those walls?

The biggest wall for most people is a lack of knowledge. "If I knew more about options, I could make money with them." Most people have never been taught anything regarding options. How can I expect it of you, or you expect it of yourself, to do something that you didn't know existed? Can you gain knowledge quickly? Yes, you can. And I don't mean just any kind of knowledge, I mean specialized knowledge. If you dig for oil where there's oil, what will you find? Oil! So, if you specialize in knowledge that makes money, what will you make? Money!

> If money is your hope for independence, you will never have it. The only real security that a man can have in this world is a reserve of knowledge, experience, and ability.
>
> *Henry Ford*

You can have a lot of knowledge about something, but what else holds us back? Fear or what I will call a lack of confidence. A lack of confidence is another wall for many people.

What do you think the scariest trade of all will be? That's right! Your first one. It was the same for everyone who has ever traded. Just like the first date, first day on the job, or the first time riding a bike. How did we conquer the fear? By doing it! What makes it a lot easier is knowing what to do, when to do it, and what to say. That increases your confidence. These reports will take you by the hand and lead you around the mines found in the minefield of options trading. Do you want to go it alone or with someone who has been across many a time?

You can have a lot of knowledge about something, and you can be full of confidence, but what else do we need to get started? Money! It is the lack of money that acts as the third wall for many people.

At our seminars across the country, people tell me all the time that they love what they learned, but they don't have any money to get started. My response is, "If you don't get some money together, will you be able to do what I'm showing you?" No. And if you continue to do what you have always done, what will you continue to get? Nothing.

The definition of crazy that I really love is: if you continue to do what you've always done but expect different results. Now, that's crazy!!

So, the question really becomes, not whether or not you have the money, but where are you going to get it? Because, if you don't get it, you can't get started. And if you can't get started, you are left with what you have. And that's what we're trying to change! We want more out of life: more money! More time with our kids!

Let me share with you a little secret: if you take time to learn how money is made, what will you start doing? Making money! If you don't take time to learn how money is made, what will be the result? Nothing.

> The American Dream is alive and well if you but take the time to learn how to get it.

Are you telling me that knowledge is the answer?! It sure is! It's knowledge that makes you money. It's knowledge that gives us confidence by knowing what to do, and when to do it. Knowledge is key!

The American Dream is alive and well if you but take the time to learn how to get it.

Congratulations on taking the first step!!

◆◆◆

This chapter contains excerpts from Steve Wirrick's Special Reports series published by Lighthouse Publishing Group, Inc. For more information on this series call 1-800-872-7411.

About The Author

teve Wirrick graduated Cum Laude from Brigham Young University. Shortly thereafter, he joined a telecommunications company, creating a seminar to market their product services throughout the country. Since that time, he has traveled the country extensively, teaching thousands of investors and entrepreneurs alike wealth enhancement and money-making strategies. He is currently working on the release of his new book, *Winning! The Only Option.*

It was during a trip home to Seattle from San Diego, California that Steve met Wade Cook. As he tells the story, it was his intention to tie his company's products and services into Wade's marketing and seminars. Instead, Wade did a lot better job of selling Steve! "It's been a wild and crazy ride getting a handle on the options market," says Steve. Adding that this knowledge has enabled him to rack up huge gains while at the same time keeping his losses to a minimum.

Success Through Technical Analysis

Gregory Witt

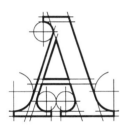s a student of the stock market I am always on the lookout for the "Holy Grail," that technique or hidden key which will allow me to detect a stock's future movement. Realistically, I know that a perfect predictive tool does not exist. However, I have discovered patterns which repeat themselves in ways that lend predictability to price movement. These patterns and indicators are used by successful investors to increase the likelihood of making money in the stock market.

If indeed, there is a holy grail or key to success in the stock market, it is knowledge. I remain solidly convinced that as an investor gains knowledge compounded by experience, the quality of their investing decisions improve. I know this has been true in my case; as I learned and applied time-tested, solid principles of technical analysis, I became more successful as an investor.

> **A professional is a man who can do his best at a time when he doesn't particularly feel like it.**
>
> *Alistair Cooke*

I have come to realize that it doesn't take a lifelong study of technical analysis or an advanced degree in statistics to bring about significant improvement in outcomes. In fact, a sound, basic knowledge of technical analysis coupled with the requisite understanding of fundamentals and other appropriate strategies can make you every bit as successful as one who devotes themselves completely to technical analysis.

My objective in the stock market has been to create wealth and financial independence. My goal? Become a millionaire through my investments in the market. As a result, my approach to technical analysis is: *what does a millionaire need to know?* There are a number of excellent books available covering technical analysis in great detail which can be valuable for further research. But I wanted to know the essentials that would make a difference in my trading *today*. This is precisely what I want to pass along to you in this chapter.

> Business is never so healthy as when, like a chicken, it must do a certain amount of scratching around for what it gets.
>
> *Henry Ford*

What is technical analysis?

Technical analysis is the study of price, volume, and market sentiment patterns as a means of determining future price movements. Technical analysis is often compared and contrasted to fundamental analysis in a way that suggests the two are contradictory or mutually exclusive. I believe successful investors learn to use the two simultaneously in a way which brings the most useful information to bear on the investment decision.

Fundamental Analysis *(What to buy)*	Technical Analysis *(When to buy)*
Financial reports	Stock Charts
Management	Trading Patterns
Marketing Strategies	Volume
Profitability	Price Trends
Price/Earnings Ratio	Market Sentiment
Products	Support/Resistance
Competition	Moving Averages

48

The underlying theory of technical analysis is that prices move in trends and patterns which are the result of many different economic, political, and psychological forces. While we can never fully predict these forces, we can come to recognize and find repetition in the resulting trends and patterns. To do this successfully is more art than science. It often requires that the investor take a position contrary to "the herd" in order to sell when the rest of the market is saying "buy."

> Success is more a function of consistent common sense than it is of genius.
>
> *An Wang*

Most charts really have very little to say; they are often ambiguous as to future movement. I have seen too many textbook and perfect charts ripped to pieces by a broader market movement. A case in point is the "mini-crash" of October 27, 1997. You can look at charts of hundreds of solid companies and find absolutely no technical indication on October 26th of what was to happen on Monday, October 27th. With that cautionary preface in mind, let's take a look at some of the technical tools I find most useful.

Dow theory

Dow theory, developed by Charles Dow and Edward Jones, is one of the oldest and best known systems used by market technicians. Its underlying principle is that the market moves in trends. The barometer created by Dow to track these trends is the Dow Jones Industrial Average and the Dow Jones Transportation Average. When these averages confirm each other, a trend is in place. That trend will remain in place until both averages reverse that trend.

Dow theory assumes that most stocks follow the underlying trend of the market. Most market observers recognize that about 70% of the movement in the price of a stock can be tied to the total market. The remaining 30% is due to supply and demand, and fundamental factors related to the stock.

Support and resistance

Most stocks fluctuate within a range. Support is the lower level of a stock's trading range at which there appears to be a limit on further price declines. Resistance is the upper level of that range at which a stock's price appears to be limited in upward movement. Support and resistance often become psychological hurdles for investors. As a stock's price increases and approaches support, investors may be inclined to sell their shares, thinking that the stock will not go any higher. Other investors may see the stock trading at a high range and will not buy because, in their mind, the stock is overvalued. As a result of these two market sentiments, the balance of trading shifts from buying to selling and the stock will indeed decline in value. The opposite occurs as a stock hits resistance.

> **Bear markets have no supports, and bull markets have no resistance.**
>
> *William F. Eng*

A stock will continue to trade within this range touching support and resistance levels. Each time a stock tests resistance by touching a previously established level of resistance, that resistance is strengthened. Those levels of support and resistance will remain in effect until market forces are compelling enough to send the price up through resistance or down through support. When this occurs there is a breakout to a higher or lower price.

Trendlines

Trends are powerful forces in the marketplace. Analyzing trends is one of the easiest technical tools to grasp. The momentum of a trend is what often drives a bull market to excessive highs and a bear market to such surprising lows. Trendlines help us identify support and resistance and enable us to make a more confident buy or sell decision.

Chart 4-1

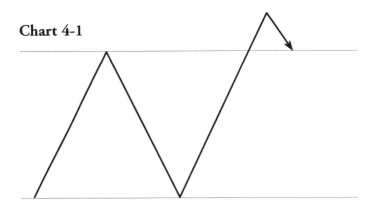

In Chart 4-1, the trendline on the bottom tracks the support level. Each time the price of the stock touches the trendline, the significance of the trend and the significance of the support level is strengthened. Eventually, the price of the stock breaks through the resistance or support level (this is referred to as a breakout by market technicians). As a stock breaks through the upper trendline, what was once resistance now becomes support. This new support level will usually be tested and established.

We often see the reverse occur as a stock price breaks down below the trendline. In this case, what was once support now becomes resistance to future upward movement.

As an investor, you need to understand where the stock is in relation to the trendline. If the stock price is on its way down to the support level (Chart 4-2), don't buy until after it has touched that support

> With enough insider information and a million dollars, you can go broke in a year.
>
> *Warren Buffett*

level, reversed the trend, and has begun its ascent back to resistance. Make the stock "prove itself" to you by touching support, reversing, and heading upwards. Remember, you don't have to be in the business of picking the market bottom or top. Assign the trend to do that job.

Chart 4-2

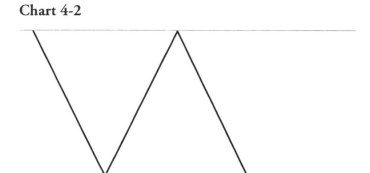

Moving averages

The most commonly used tool in working with trendlines is a moving average. Most stock charting software includes tools for plotting moving averages. A moving average is created by averaging the closing price for a set number of previous days. A chart showing moving averages tends to smooth out the fluctuations found in daily stock charts and gives a more even display of the stock's movement. While I find a moving average to be a useful tool in the analysis of most trending stocks, I find it to be of limited value in working with rolling stocks. The more volatile and fast-moving the stock, the less useful a moving average is.

> Great things are not done by impulse but by a series of small things brought together.
>
> *Vincent van Gogh*

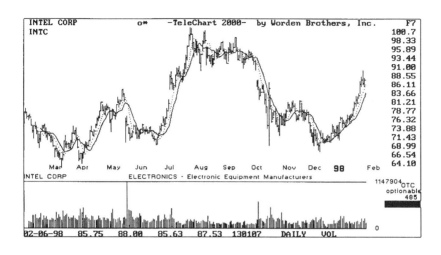

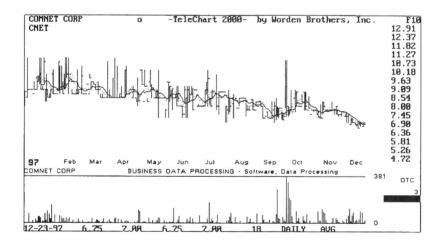

The previous charts show both the benefits of using a moving average for most heavily traded stocks, and the limitations of using a moving average for most low priced rolling stocks. Both charts show the price of the stock and two superimposed moving averages, a five-day moving average (shown in the dotted line) and a nine-day moving average (shown in the smoother solid line).

On the chart for Intel (INTC), a strong upward trend is manifest as the shorter term average (the dotted line) moves away from and above the longer term (solid line) average. The crossing of the two averages indicates a trend reversal. On the downturn, the shorter term average falls below the longer term average as the stock's price falls. Most experienced investors would want to see the downward trend reversed before buying the stock.

Volume

Volume measures the number of shares traded during a specified time frame. Since price movement is a function of supply and demand, volume is an important indicator in measuring market interest and its relation to price movement.

> **Many of life's failures are people who did not realize how close they were to success when they gave up.**
>
> *Thomas Edison*

When the price of a stock increases on expanding volume, that is a good signal indicating that a positive trend is in place. A price increase on declining volume suggests that the trend is losing momentum. A reversal or downturn could be imminent.

Similarly, a downtrend on increasing volume is a bearish signal. The downtrend is not likely to reverse until volume pulls back and support is established.

Stochastics

Stochastics come from the Greek word *stochastes* meaning "diviner." Stochastics is a statistical tool used by market technicians in determining whether a stock's price is overbought or oversold. In the stock market, stochastics uses a stock's historic trading range and price movement as a basis for indicating the direction of the stock's future movement. A charting service which provides stochastic analysis is a powerful tool for identifying the right buying and selling opportunity. Stochastics is most effective with a rolling stock, as opposed to a more trending stock.

Stochastics shows where the price of the stock is trading within a given range. The theory behind the indicator, which was invented by George Lane, is that prices tend to close near the upper end of a trading range during an uptrend. As the trend matures, the tendency for prices to close away from the higher end of the trading range becomes more pronounced. In a downward trending market, the reverse is true.

> I like to buy stocks when the bears are giving them away.
>
> *Warren Buffett*

Stochastics help us determine whether a stock is overbought or oversold. When the stochastics cross up through the 80% line, it is considered overbought. Below the 20% line is oversold. When the near term moving average line crosses up and through the longer term moving average line, a buy signal is produced. Conversely, when an overbought stochastic turns down through its moving average, a sell signal is produced.

In most charting software, the sampling time period can be determined by the user. One suggested setting which gives a good, near term reading is a sampling period of 14, with moving averages of seven and nine. For Telechart 2000® users, go to the Indicator menu and bring up Stochastics. A bow will appear and allow you to enter a number for period. Enter 14 for period, and seven for moving average. A second window will appear. In this window enter nine for moving average and two for last indicator (placing the graph in the lower window) You should set each moving average for a different color so that it is clearly evident when the near term moving average crosses up and through the longer term moving average.

Balance of Power™

Balance of Power is the exclusive intellectual property of Worden Brothers Inc. and is a technical indicator featured on their Telechart 2000® and Telechart Professional charting software.

Balance of Power (BOP) doesn't tell you if a stock will go up or down. What it does tell us is if the current trading of stock is characterized by systematic buying (accumulation) or systematic selling (distribution). BOP brings out hidden patterns of *informed* buying and selling. It is based on the premise that if you invest consistently in the same direction as informed money, your chances of success will increase significantly.

For convenience, BOP is plotted in color. Green signifies dominant buying. Red signifies dominant selling. When BOP is close to the zero line, revealing no clear dominance of either buying or selling, it is plotted in yellow.

BOP is described as a "trend quality indicator," that is, it tells you something about the quality of the underlying trend. It will help you determine whether the supply and demand balance will be in your favor. It will help you spot changes of character in a stock's action.

If you are considering the purchase of a particular stock but aren't happy with the current price, just wait a minute.

Market Maxim

The single most definitive and valuable characteristic of BOP is a pronounced ability to contradict price movement. Thus, while the price is attaining new highs, BOP may very well be attaining new lows. It is not unusual for BOP to move in the exact opposite direction of price.

BOP is not a short-term timing aid. BOP shows patterns of systematic long-term oriented accumulation and distribution. It doesn't tell you when the price will respond to the pattern or even if it will respond. But common sense tells us consistent accumulation will likely result in a higher price.

A few days of yellow BOP should not be regarded as an interruption of an established pattern of accumulation, especially if this occurs during a period of short term price weakness.

The MoneyStream™

The Cumulative MoneyStream (CMS) is also the exclusive intellectual property of the Worden Brothers Inc. It is a cumulative price/volume indicator which lends itself better to precise timing than BOP. In reading the CMS chart, the key is to look for divergences, or differences, between price line and the CMS line.

Important divergences can be seen at a glance by comparing the automatic linear regression lines on the CMS graph to those on the price graph. If the CMS regression lines are sloping upward at greater angles than those of the price, the

I'd be a bum on the street with a tin cup if the markets were always efficient.

Warren Buffett

message is bullish, and vice versa. If, for example, the short-term white regression line is going up at a steeper angle than the corresponding regression line on the price graph, the indication is that price will rise to meet the MoneyStream.

CMS has some predictive power, although it seems to work best when used in conjunction with BOP. CMS and BOP are based on entirely different concepts and sometimes they disagree completely. The idea is to wait for mutual confirmation and situations when both

CMS and BOP are giving the same signal. Like many technical indicators, CMS and BOP tend to be more predictive with heavily traded large company stocks where the market is often most efficient.

Successful investing requires knowledge, action, and commitment. Learning the right strategies will take you a long way on the path to success. Having a working knowledge of these technical indicators combined with the ability to use principles of fundamental analysis will make a noticeable difference in the quality of your investment decisions. Technical and fundamental analysis are the basic tools used by all successful investors. Learn to use these tools well and your results will speak for themselves.

If football taught me anything about business it is that you win the game one play at a time.

Fran Tarkenton

◆◆◆

This chapter contains excerpts from Greg Witt's Book, *Rolling Stocks*, published by Lighthouse Publishing Group, Inc. This book will be available soon in better bookstores.

About The Author

reg Witt comes to the stock market with a background as a business owner and entrepreneur. He is the author of *Rolling Stocks* from Lighthouse Publishing Group, Inc. He is an active trader in the stock market and particularly enjoys teaching Wade Cook's strategies in the Wall Street Workshop.

He has a masters degree in Organizational Behavior from Brigham Young University.

He is an avid traveler and is frequently found conducting historical and archeological tours of Central America, Israel, and Egypt.

He lives in Provo, Utah with his wife Elain and their five children.

Succeed With Options

Tim Semingson

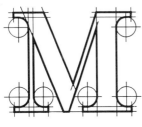any have likened the stock market to a beast. Wild, unpredictable, and yes, even dangerous. It seems as though the market has a mind of its own. Usually, those claiming to have power to predict the market or time the market are wrong. In fact, over the last 10 years, out of all the mutual fund managers, only about 19% have effectively outperformed the market. This means that 81% of mutual fund managers that move the majority of money in the stock market have been wrong. They have underperformed the Dow Jones 30 industrial average. They have underperformed the Standard & Poors 500 Index. The Dow 30 and the S&P 500 have performed at approximately 10.7% per year since their inceptions. If we are paying money managers good money to invest for us and they are underperforming the entire market, then maybe we should look elsewhere for a method or strategy that is not only effective in matching the markets performance, but in outperforming it as well.

> Security is mostly a superstition. It does not exist in nature ... Life is either a daring adventure or nothing.
>
> *Helen Keller*

A way to do this is to recognize the movements of the market, and when I say recognize, I don't mean being able to predict the movements of the market. I'm talking about spotting market momentum. I'm talking about recognizing a beast that is coming at you with sharp teeth and claws and ready to tear your head off. I'm talking about respecting the power in the market. But, I'm also talking about being able to capitalize on this movement. I'm talking about sometimes stepping out of the way so that you don't get hurt. I'm talking about sometimes being able to attack from a contrarian standpoint. And, I'm talking about other times being able to aggressively follow the momentum and possibly deliver a blow from the backside.

> Power is not revealed by striking hard or often, but by striking true.
>
> *Honoré de Balzac*

This can be done a number of different ways through investing in options. People that buy stocks have to be *right* in order to be profitable. In other words, anyone buying a stock must see performance in a stock in one direction, and that means price moving up or they stand to post a loss. Now, patience is a virtue in stocks. Meaning, we don't have to be *right in a specific period of time* to be profitable. As long as we don't sell at a loss, eventually, we may end up being right. The question is: "how long is eventually?" Do we have enough time to wait for a stock to go up? Do we have enough time to wait for a portfolio to go up? Do we have enough time to wait if it is under-performing the most basic industrial groups, the Dow 30?

The Dow Jones Industrial Average is made up of 30 stocks with huge monthly capitalization. These stocks represent a relatively broad compilation of industries in the stock market. The Standard & Poors 500 index is quite a bit more broad representing 500 companies in every imaginable industry group. But performance is relatively the same between these two groups (1.7% annually). Some years we may see better performance, some years we may see under-performance. But over all, if we can not only match the performance of the market, but outperform the market, we are in the top 20 percentile of all money managers. These are money managers that manage millions and millions, even billions, of dollars. These are the institutional investors—managing mutual funds. We're talking about financial institutions, banks, even insurance companies where the majority of money is placed in investment portfolios.

But, if we could learn not only to recognize market movement, but to capitalize on the market movement, by recognizing what these money managers are doing with their money that is helping to cause prices to either accelerate or decelerate, to advance or decline, then why can't we also implement a strategy that will only increase our percentage success ratio?

> In selecting the soundest financial investments, the question of when to buy is far more important than what to buy.
>
> *Roger W. Babson*

We need to start by considering that of all the world markets, about 43.7% of stocks are made up of U.S. stocks. This means that over half of the world's stocks aren't available on the U.S. stock markets. We need to look at the world economy as a whole. Maybe we need to research how foreign currencies work in conjunction with our dollar. How is the falling dollar balanced by world economy? If the value of the dollar is falling, how is it reflected in other currencies? If we see a coffee shortage in South America, how will it affect prices of coffee, and more importantly, how will it affect the prices of stocks that buy that coffee at a wholesale price and sell it at a retail price to its customers? How does strong a U.S. economy, or fear of inflation, or a rising interest rate affect the U.S. stock market? By trying to understand world economy; that is, the stocks, commodities, and currencies, we may be able to get a little better insight into how money flows globally. If we have a little better insight into how money flows globally, we may be able to funnel that broad information down a little bit narrower.

We may now be able to focus on one area, whether it is stocks, commodities, or currencies. We may even be able to funnel that area down if we're talking about stocks and we see momentum in the U.S. stock market in one direction or the other. Some say that about 70% of the mutual fund managers, the institutional investors, the banks, and the insurance companies are program traders, capitalizing on buy and sell signals, capitalizing on money flow and on supply and demand. They are capitalizing on support and resistance levels where stocks typically will

You can make even a parrot into a learned economist by teaching him two words: supply and demand.

Anonymous

trade, capitalizing on moving averages of price, and on convergence and divergence. We, then, may be able to grasp a piece of the momentum, but also increase our chances for success by recognizing an industry, a sector, or an industrial group that has more specific momentum—maybe an industry group or sector that is outperforming the overall market, that has momentum, but has exaggerated momentum. Then maybe we can funnel this down even more and focus on an individual stock that is not only outperforming the market momentum, but is outperforming its industry group's momentum, and now we are at a point where we can apply a strategy to capitalize for profits.

We can not only ride the market momentum, but we can ride an industry's momentum and we can ride stock momentum. We can also ride the momentum that is self-fulfilling in nature through momentum of the program traders. Applying a proper strategy that would give us a cushion to where we not only we have to be *right* in order to be profitable, as we do when we buy stocks, but we could even be wrong and still be profitable in our trade. *This can only be done in options.*

How many times have we gotten up in the morning and said to ourselves, "The stock market is going to rally today" or "the stock market is going to bank today?" Out of those times when we predicted what way the market would go, in the course of one day, how may times were we right and how many times were we wrong? I would venture to say that most people are wrong more than they are right. See, this is the beauty of riding momentum. This is the beauty of not having to be right. We can ride a percentage, albeit big or small, of the market's momentum. We can ride a percentage of an industry's momentum. We can ride a percentage of a stock's momentum and when we are applying the proper strategy, we can even be wrong and still be profitable. Though, a momentum is recognizable, the program traders are a large part of the reason that momentum is created. This is supply and demand at its very best.

Let's start by getting a grip on our own economy. We have certain economic reports that come out monthly and investors who will react accordingly. Sometimes, stock prices trade more based on public perception than they do on actual fact. This means the CPI, (Consumer Price Index) or PPI, (Producer Price Index) or the labor report, may come out. Investors will interpret that information; more specifically, they will speculate on how others will react (by others I mean the federal chairman) and how he will either raise interest rates or lower interest rates based on what the economy is doing. If consumer or producer price indexes are positive or higher than expected, then that means the economy is stronger than expected. A strong economy, by any means, is good news. Unfortunately, too strong of an economy would cause interest rates to be raised. Interest rates being raised means that it would cost companies more money to borrow on short term loans. That in turn, means that their earnings would not be as high as previously

> To most of us, the leading economic indicator is our bank account.
>
> *Joe Moore*

expected. So, lower earnings would cause poorer performance in stocks. Poorer performance in stocks would cause people to sell stocks, possibly funneling their money, or channeling their money, over into an interest rate sensitive investment.

The majority of people that would react to news like this aren't the small time investors. They aren't what is known as the float of the shares note standing in a company. These people minimally push prices of stock. Again, the big players are not only the program traders, but the institutional investors. These people are the ones who dictate whether there is more supply or demand for a stock. Stock prices trade according to supply and demand just like any other business. The greater the demand per stock, the greater the accumulation of a stock and the higher the prices will be pushed. The greater supply of a stock or the greater sell off of a stock, the lower the prices will be pressured. The key is recognizing the reaction to certain economic reports and being able to capitalize on them, or being able to step out of the way if you aren't sure, yet, how these economic reports effect the stock market.

With unemployment reports, we see that a higher unemployment rate is actually good news. One would think that this is bad news because fewer Americans are employed. But overall, more employed Americans means that the economy is stronger. Again, it raises the question in investors minds: "is inflation too high?" Will interest rates be raised to lower that inflation, to lower the growing economy? Housing starts could start a whole cyclone of events if they are higher than projected, higher than the same quarter last year, or higher than some little person or analyst had thought that they would be. This also would represent a stronger economy. This also would raise fear in

> **The rate of unemployment is 100 percent if it's you who is unemployed.**
>
> *David L. Kurtz*

66

people's minds of whether or not inflation was growing too rapidly. Would interest rates be adjusted to lower that pace? Ultimately, the possibility of interest rates being raised is a report that might be the most crucial of all. Periodically, we see that there will be a report. Will the federal government raise interest rates, lower interest rates, or will they let interest rates remain unchanged?

> **A frightened captain makes a frightened crew.**
>
> *Lister Sinclair*

Exactly, how severely will the public react to these reports? What factors are also in place that might contribute to those reports? What is going on in the world economy? By watching the world a little bit closer, we may eventually be able to recognize market trends when they are in motion and by using the right strategy at the right time, we can do what everyone has set out to do: Make more money.

On even a broader scope, if we are trying to track or capitalize on the entire movement on a market, whether it be the U.S. stock market or international markets, we may consider a couple of things. First of all, if we're capitalizing on the U.S. stock market, the Standard & Poors 500 Index represents a wide group of industries or sector in the market. We may capitalize on the performance of a market trend in the U.S. stock market by buying into a company that purchases shares of all the companies in the Standard & Poors 500 Index. This would be known as Standard & Poors Depository Receipts or commonly known as SPiDeRs. The ticker symbol for this company would be SPY. It trades at about one-tenth of the valuation of the Standard & Poors 500 Index. By buying stock in SPY, we can effectively participate in the momentum of the overall market in U.S. stocks.

On a broader scale, maybe we would like to capitalize on momentum in international stocks. Since the U.S. stock market only makes up for 43.7% of the total overall market, let's take a look at the other 56.3% of foreign stocks. Consider the Morgan Stanley Capital National Country Index, MSCI. This would be an index designed to capitalize on movement in a particular foreign country's prices of stocks. But similar to SPiDeRs, there is another way to capitalize on the momentum on these foreign stocks. They are called WEBS, World Equity Benchmark Shares. Each country abroad may have a series of securities traded on the American stock exchange that we can actually participate in purchasing. WEBS are designed for 17 different countries. Each WEB is designed to U.S. investors exposure to specific international equity markets through diversified portfolios of stocks for each foreign country selected. WEBS are traded as stocks. We buy shares in WEBS for any of the 17 foreign countries. They're marketable and provide dividend yield, and sometimes, spectacular total returns. By tracking the performance of each foreign company and how it fared, or whether it storms through hard times, we may spot momentum trends that outperform the overall markets. For example, in light of the October 28, 1997 crash, as some would call it, or decline of the Dow Jones Industrial Average of 554 points. In researching the international stocks performance, we find that there are certain countries with a list of securities attached to them that have rebounded rather nicely from this crash. As of November 3, 1997, which was only one week after the 550 point drop, certain countries have not only posted positive gains for the prior year, but some have posted phenomenal gains not only in price but in dividend yield for spectacular total returns.

> **Call it what you will, incentives are the only way to make people work harder.**
>
> *Nikita Khrushchev*

Here are index series posted from various countries for one year:

Country	Total Percentage Return
Spain	36.68
France	14.06
Germany	19.68
Italy	35.21
Mexico	35.91
Netherlands	27.9
Sweden	21.67
Switzerland	28.55
United Kingdom	29.39

Now, there are other countries that have showed positive gains as well. Many have gained beyond the average of the Standard & Poors 500 Index or the Dow Jones Industrial Average which is 10.7% annually.

On a broad scope we can capitalize on entire market momentum, not only in the United States but in foreign countries as well by using SPiDeRs and WEBS. These are not optionable. They should be considered for longer term growth and momentum trends. But on the shorter term, we need to look at capitalizing on momentum with leverage. Leverage means a smaller amount of money on the table at risk with greater possible rates of return, and this can be done by using options spreads. Option spreads will enable us to generate immediate income on options that we have purchased, lower our risk and also provide a cushion where we can be profitable in a trade no matter if the stock goes up, stays where it is in terms of price, or even drops in price. In other words, by using option spreads, we increase our odds to where we can even be wrong and still be profitable.

Leverage means a smaller amount of money on the table at risk with greater possible rates of return, and this can be done by using options spreads.

For a larger part of our portfolio, yes, maybe we should look at owning stock which provides solidity, support, stability and longer term growth. But for an additional part of our portfolio, maybe we should consider generating immediate income using options to lower our risk rather than having our money at 100% risk and also providing a cushion for profitability. By watching the entire world markets, we can capitalize on momentum in a number of different countries, international stocks or in U.S. stocks. But again, by funneling down to spot industry groups or sectors with specific momentum; and then funneling down even further to spot stocks, individual stocks, within those sectors that have outperforming momentum, we can apply a strategy known as option spreads to post immediate profits, to elevate our rates of return and create monthly, even weekly cash flow in our accounts.

The market may, indeed, be a beast—wild, unpredictable and dangerous. Whether we are talking about the currencies markets, the commodities markets, or the stock markets, we have a choice laid out before us. We can use fundamentals to our advantage, and we can use technical analysis or charts to our advantage. But applying the proper strategy at that proper time on the proper stock may be the greatest dilemma of all. Let's take a look and dedicate the rest of this book to strategies that will enhance our cash flow, lower our risk and provide a cushion to where we can even be wrong and still win. Diversification is great for a well balanced portfolio. It would hedge us against a declining U.S. dollar by providing growth in overseas funds. It would balance our risk to the point where we would be able to sleep at night. So, by using SPiDeRs and WEBS, we can match the performance of the U.S. stock market, and we may be able to out perform the performance of the U.S. stock market by using international stocks.

> All strategy depends on competition.
>
> *Bruce D. Henderson*

Where will the money come from to invest in the U.S. and foreign stock markets? Where will these profits be generated from with a minimal amount of risk? That's what we are about to explore: how to generate profits with immediate cash flow and to lower our risk in options.

◆ ◆ ◆

This chapter contains excerpts from Tim Semingson's Special Reports series published by Lighthouse Publishing Group, Inc. For more information on this series call 1-800-872-7411.

About The Author

im Semingson, born in Wisconsin, is currently an international speaker in financial education. Since attending college, he has spent years teaching various financial seminars. The topics range from basic fundamental and technical analysis to advanced stock and option trading strategies.

His upcoming book, written for the average investor, is built on the belief that self money management can lead to financial independence. The author's current research involves world markets in relation to trading index options.

The CEO of two corporations, Tim Semingson is the father of two boys, and resides in the Pacific Northwest.

Covered Calls And Success

Debbie Losse

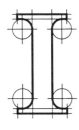f you are like me, the word "stock market" is one of these words that was used only on the "Lifestyles of the Rich and Famous!" Pork bellies, commodities, and all sorts of other unfamiliar words seem to attach themselves to those two words. Actually, when you break down those two words, they aren't as scary. "Stock" reminds me of a big soup pot and "market" is where I seem to go every other day to fill up my two teenage kids. However, that is not what is meant when stock market is mentioned. Whenever it

> I have always said that if I were a rich man I would employ a professional praiser.
>
> *Sir Osbert Sitwell*

came up in a conversation, I would politely find something else to do. My husband had a little better insight and he thought I could comprehend, so he finally persuaded me to attend a seminar that could give me a better outlook on what the stock market was all about. What I found was the fear that haunts most Americans today, the fear of the unknown. In this chapter I would like to help you overcome that fear and start you on the path of knowledge and financial independence, all in one shot.

Let's deal with the fear that all of us go through. Most people have a tendency to dwell only on the negative side of an issue:

"I don't know where to start. I don't have the education. I don't have time to watch the stock market every day. I don't know a good company from a bad company. I don't want to lose all of the money it took me a lifetime to build. I don't want to start all over if I fail." These are very valid concerns.

On the positive side of the coin, just think of your financial independence, going to work because you *want* to and not because you *have* to, doing things with your family, teaching your children how to have financial security, being able to help the unfortunate, giving someone or some family the chance to start a new life, knowing that the education you receive can not be taken from you.

> The person who knows *how* will always have a job. The person who knows *why* will always be his boss.
>
> *Diane Ravitch*

Almost every major breakthrough is the result of a courageous break with traditional ways of thinking. For example, around 500 years ago, European maps depicted a limited and flat earth. Then an expert navigator and courageous seaman named Christopher Columbus challenged the conventional way of sailing and set out to discover a new route to the Indies. He failed to discover the Indies, but he certainly changed the map and changed history. In attending a banquet in his honor, a jealous man asked him, "Had you not discovered the Indies, are there not other men in Spain who would have been able to accomplish the same feat?"

Columbus made no reply but took an egg and asked the heckler to make it stand on end. After all attempts had failed, he tapped it on the table, denting one end, and left it standing.

"We all could have done it that way!" the jealous man charged.

Columbus replied, "Yes, if you had only known how. And once I showed you the way to the New World, nothing was easier than to follow it." Most of the time we can't embrace a new paradigm (way of thinking) until we let go of the old ones.

What you need, as I did, was someone who will walk you down the path addressing all your issues and showing you that fear is often exaggerated in our minds. We sometimes make the answers out to be more complicated than they truly need to be. It reminds me of a poem entitled "Life's Contract." It goes like this:

> I bargained with life for a penny,
> And life would pay me no more
> However I begged at evening
> When I counted my scanty score.
> For life is a just employer.
> It pays you what you ask.
> But once you set the price
> Then you must bear the task.
> I worked for a menial hire
> Only to learn dismayed
> That any wage I asked of life
> Life would have willingly paid.
> —Anonymous

Overcoming old paradigms is a large part of knowing who you are and what you want to accomplish.

We work to become, not to acquire.

Elbert Hubbard

I attended a seminar at which both Wade Cook and Steve Wirrick spoke concerning the fears and issues relating to the stock market. After two days of invaluable training, I looked at my husband and stated, "What took you so long to get me here? Do you know where we could be if I had had this education and information sooner?"

Of course, as he always does, he humored me by smiling and saying "Yes, dear." We need to step out of our comfort zone and experience what life has to offer. The offer might just be what we need.

> Nothing is so powerful as an insight into human nature...what compulsions drive a man, what instincts dominate his action...if you know these things about a man you can touch him at the core of his being.
>
> *William Bernbach*

You don't need to be a rocket scientist, or a high school graduate to obtain the skills needed to succeed in the stock market. We can break out of our comfort zones and increase our knowledge one day at a time. We can't exercise thirty minutes without killing ourselves if we haven't worked up to it. We need to build up gradually.

It's the same way with the stock market. Work up to the more difficult strategies by finding one that has few risks involved. One of the most conservative strategies is writing a covered call. After going through and understanding this concept, the sky becomes the limit! If getting anywhere from 13 to 35% *monthly* returns excites you, then hold on, 'cause here we go.

In stock market terms, the word writing means to sell, and covered means owning a stock. A broker can tell you if the stock is optionable, meaning that you can sell someone else the right to buy your stock from you at a later date. If so, you might be able to collect extra cash right now. Someone will pay you a premium, for the right to buy *your* stock, at *your* price, on or before the expiration date! Isn't that a great deal? Before we go any further, there are a few terms that you should become familiar with.

One **contract** equals 100 shares (so two contracts would be 200 shares).

The **expiration date** is the third Friday of each month.

The price you are willing to sell for is called a **strike price**.

The **premium** is set by the market makers and clears in one day. In other words, the day after you sell your call, the premium is in your account and is yours to keep no matter what!

Let's give you an example so that everything fits into place. Years ago Wade Cook had accumulated 3,800 shares of Novell Computer, Inc. (NOVL). The stock had done several stock splits (which we really like and will tell you more about later) so he figured while it was down around $16 to $19 he would load up and wait for it to climb back to around $60 or so, like it had done before. Well guess what didn't happen? You got it. It did not pop back up like he thought it would. After waiting forever, he got upset. So he told his broker, "When the stock gets up to $20 per share, sell all my shares."

> No price is too low for a bear or too high for a bull.
>
> *Market Maxim*

His broker said, "If you are going to do that, why don't you write a covered call on them?" Wade asked him to explain. "Right now you can sell someone else the right to buy your shares for $20 each, next month. You'll collect the premium for selling him this right. If he chooses to exercise it, you'll also sell the stock for $20, only it will be a month from now. So you'll make money twice."

Wade asked his stockbroker how much he would receive. The broker checked his computer for options and told him the next month call options, with a strike price (the price he agreed to sell at) had a bid of $1. Since he had 3,800 shares, that would generate $3,800 in his account the next day.

Wade asked, "You mean I can get $3,800 cash in my account tomorrow for selling the right to someone to buy my Novell shares within the next month (remember on or before the 3rd Friday of the month) at $20?"

"That's right."

"This is a no-brainer, do it!"

The stock was bouncing around between $18 and $21, however, that first month it was around $20.50 on the expiration date, and Wade was "called out" (someone exercised his right to buy the stock at $20) of 1,100 shares. Why he did not get called out of all the shares is one of those mysteries of the market. If it's close to the strike price, sometimes you get called out, sometimes you don't. To recap, he received $3,800 in premium and $22,000 ($20 x 1,100 shares).

> The man who will use his skill and constructive imagination to see how much he can give for a dollar instead of how little he can give for a dollar is bound to succeed.
>
> *Henry Ford*

Well, he still had 2,700 shares left, so what do you think he did? He called again and the options for the next month were $1.25. He sold the call and received $3,375 (2,700 x $1.25). He was called out of 1,000 shares. So, not only did he get the $3,375, he also received $20,000 (1,000 x $20). He continued to sell the calls until all the shares he had were gone. This was his first experience writing a covered call. He was starting to get a glimpse of a whole new cash flow machine using the stock market.

Here are a couple of points you should remember:

1. American style options (the only type we use in this country) can be exercised any time on or before the expiration date.

2. You don't have to do anything to sell your stock. You will find out the Monday following the third Friday if your stock got called out. It all happens on computers with a lottery-type system. A confirmation slip will be sent showing "account assigned."

3. If you sell your call, that stock is then tied up until the expiration date.

To really excel with our covered call formula, you need to engage in margin trading. What the heck is that? Simply put, you only have to put up half the money and the broker puts up the other half in purchasing stock. If you needed $10,000 to initiate a deal, you would have to put $5,000 in your brokerage account and your broker would "lend" you the other $5,000. Why does he do this? Because you're a great person and he wants to be Mr. Nice Guy? I don't think so! He does it for two reasons: a bigger commission and the margin interest.

You will find in working with the stock market that there are givens, the price of doing business. Don't get me wrong. We still need to be conscious of our costs and need to negotiate the best deal; just know that commissions and margins are just a small fraction of the total package. We are continually telling people to quit tripping over pennies on their way to dollars. If you use the covered call strategy of investing

> **Dollars do better if they are accompanied by sense.**
>
> *Earl Riney*

effectively, commissions and margin interest will be peanuts compared to the profits. Commissions on options are cheaper than those on stocks anyway.

Levitz Furniture (LFI) is another example I would like to share with you. It was rumored that Levitz was to be taken over. The stock was at $7. Wade bought 1,000 shares for $3,500 (10 contracts x $7 divided by 2 for margin=$3,500). He then sold the call for 50¢ on a $7.50 strike price (the price he agreed to sell at), which put $500 (1000 x .50 = $500) into his account. The stock went up to $8 and he was called out (sold the stock) making another 50¢ a share.

Let's stop here a moment and figure our rate of return. Why? This will be an important step in determining what type of stock you will be looking at when purchasing.

You calculate a rate of return (yield) by dividing the cash you receive, or the cash in (profits) by the cash you spend, or the cash out (investment).

Cash in
Cash out
Taking our example, you take:
$500
$3,500

A billion here, a billion there, and pretty soon you're talking about real money.

attributed to
Everett M. Dirksen

Move over 6% CD! This was a two-week return! If you take 26 two-week periods times 14%, you get an annualized return of 364%. Can you handle that type of return? I bet you could learn to live with it.

One American tradition is to think annually: annual this and annual that. Remember you need to get out of the comfort zones set by someone else and take charge. It's almost like un-brainwashing yourself and setting up a new set of rules. Think in terms of weekly or monthly cash flow. When this paradigm is adopted, your life will never be the same.

> If stock market experts were so expert, they would be buying stocks, not selling advice.
>
> *Norman Augustine*

So what are the ingredients to Wade Cook's covered call formula? There are three that are pretty important:

1. Use margin (unless the market is declining). You can't do margin in an IRA, except in special circumstances. However, our company, Wade Cook Seminars, Inc., sets up pension plans for people and businesses. We set up 401(k)s, Keogh plans, and corporate pension plans (corporate plans being more effective). Our master plan, approved by the IRS, allows you to trade on margin. This is an important point to bring up. If you set up a pension account through us, you will be able to trade on margin. Also, you will be in full control, with no one touching your money but you. Call our office for more information at 1-800-872-7411.

2. The best price range for stock is in the $5 to $18 range. The reason is, if you buy a stock for $6.50 and write a $7.50 call, you'll receive 75¢ to $1.25 for the premium. If you buy a stock for $48 and write a $50 call, you'll receive 75¢ to $1.25. If you buy a stock for $98 and write a $100 call, you'll receive 75¢ to $1.25. The point is, the call premiums are about the same if you're selling close to the next strike price. You can buy a lot more stock at $9 than at $99 per share.

3. You will need a certain volatility to make this work really well. You see, a key to this process is to buy low and sell high.

In business terms that would be to buy wholesale and sell retail, and in covered call terms, that would be to buy the stock on dips (weakness) and sell the call on strength.

Side Notes:

1. The assumptions above (75¢ to $1.25) could have been 50¢ to $2, but they are similar all the way to the higher-priced stocks.

2. We assume a one-month expiration date. Why would you go out two or three months? The premiums may be larger, but you need to remember that your stock is tied up for that period of time.

3. We actually like stocks in the $9 to $12 range. Why? There just aren't that many stocks in the $5 to $8 range.

So your next questions might be "How do you find good candidates for covered calls?" Here are a few ways to find them.

> The trouble with research is that it tells you what people were thinking about yesterday, not tomorrow. It's like driving a car using a rear-view mirror.
>
> *Bernard Loomis*

1. Read. I start at the front page of the business section (once I finish the comic page) and read. News helps create volatility. I call my broker with a list of candidates and we discuss prices. He knows what I like.

2. Share information. When teaching at a seminar, our students and clients continually share information they have found on stocks, either in person or by using our WIN subscription internet web site.

3. Use brokers. My brokers also call me with covered call possibilities. Many stockbrokers know about writing covered calls, and some are quite knowledgeable.

Writing covered calls actually generates two different types of income:

1. The premium for selling the call. When does it hit your account? You are right, the next day. Could you use the money for other things? Yes!

2. Capital gains money. If, for example, you were to buy a stock at $10 and sell it for $12.50 or $15, the difference would be entered as a capital gain. This money then hits your account three days after the sell date.

There could be a loss if the stock went down and you chose to sell at the lower price, but the capital loss would be mitigated by any premium that you received. Just in case you forgot, you get to keep the premium whether you sell the stock or not.

I think you are ready to comprehend a couple of new phrases used in the stock market. They are:

1. Out of the money (calls)
2. At the money
3. In the money

Before I get started, however, take a deep breath and don't have heart palpitations. Remember, don't make this hard.

Okay, let's review "out of the money." If the stock price is below the strike price, it is said to be out of the money. If the stock is at $9 and you have a $10 strike price, it would be out of the money by $1.

> The will to win is not nearly as important as the will to prepare to win.
>
> *Bobby Knight*

We make most of our profits by buying stocks slightly out of the money and waiting a short time to sell the option and receive a premium.

"At the money" is when the stock price and the strike price are the same. For covered call writing, one important concept is to purchase the stock below the strike price and hope to sell the option when the strike price gets close to being at the money, or even better, in the money.

When the stock price is more than the strike price, the stock is "in the money." A stock priced at $11.50 is in the money by $1.50 on a $10 strike price.

What would it be if your stock price was $11.50 and had a $12.50 strike price? See how smart you now have become. Your answer, out of the money, was correct.

> There are three ingredients in the good life: learning, earning, and yearning.
>
> *Christopher Morley*

What would happen if we turned writing covered calls into a business, with cash flow constantly being generated?

Here are some things that could happen:

1. We get really good at it. The task stays the same; our ability is what gets better.

2. We keep building. We're taking the cash flow, adding it to the account, which produces larger margin capabilities, and more actual cash to work with.

3. Our brokers learn what we are looking for. It's a two-way street. We can grow a lot faster together than we can apart.

4. Get to do things we want to do. Have you ever wanted to call your office and say, "It's too pretty to come to work." With a covered call business we dictate where our time can be spent.

There are around 11 different strategies that our company teaches in the Wall Street Workshop. I have only shared one of those with you. There are even variations on this strategy. But one thing you need to remember is: it only takes one to start making money. As you can see, you don't need a high school or college degree to understand and excel with this one simple cash-flow strategy. Remember we talked about taking that first step out of our comfort zone? Here is your chance. By taking the time and energy to read this book, you have indeed started down a different path.

About The Author

ebbie Losse was raised in Seattle, Washington. She is the eldest of seven. Her father worked for Boeing. She holds an associates degree in Business Management. Her husband, Doyle, and she are former business owners of 17 years in the oil and gas industry, and a manager for major aerospace company. After attending a seminar herself, she became one of the first financial seminar speakers for Wade Cook Seminars and is current Director of Product Development where she has created fun, new products for the benefit of our students.

As a child she wanted to be a policewoman, limousine driver, or a flower shop owner. By the age of 24, she had owned a limo company, owned a florist shop, and had spent extensive hours as a volunteer working to help children involved in violent situations. She has dedicated her life to teaching youth in the areas of karate (she currently holds a brown belt) and stock market strategies. Currently she is working on a pilot program for high schoolers called "Kids "IN" Business." A program where business men and woman go into classrooms and teach students "Business 101."

Her interests include family, church, reading, and snowmobiling. Living in the beautiful Cascade Mountains with her husband of 26 years, Doyle, and they are the proud parents of Renon and Trevor.

"Be sure to learn how to love yourself so that you can love others."

Puts Can Be Successful

Rich Simmons

uts are not always negative. Usually the mention of the word "puts" conjures up a great deal of negativity. As we know, puts are traditionally used as a hedge against stocks losing value. For example, you own stock that has a current value of $54. Let's say the company reports earnings which do not meet analysts' expectations. Such news will

> Usually the mention of the word "puts" conjures up a great deal of negativity.

likely cause the market price of the stock to drop. If you own the stock, you can: 1) hold it and hope that it rebounds; 2) sell it for a loss; or 3) buy insurance in the form of a put option. The first two choices are undesirable because they result in sacrifice of either time (similar to the wasted time of holding an undesirable stock) or money (like taking a loss on the sale of the stock). Let's consider the third choice and see if it provides a better result.

The holder of a put option has the right, not the obligation, to put (or sell) stock at a set price. You spend money for the put in a way similar to the deductible on your auto insurance policy. If you get in an accident, all you pay is the deductible. The insurance company pays the rest, regardless of how badly the vehicle is damaged. Similarly, if your stock drops in price, all you pay is the price of the put.

You are protected from further loss because you have the right to sell your stock at the strike price, regardless of the market price of the stock. You can choose your deductible. If you want greater protection, buy an in the money put (say, $60 or $55). For a lower deductible, buy an out of the money put ($50 or $45). Either way, the cost of the put is solely for the purpose of cutting your losses rather than generating any real profit. It is a defensive strategy that rarely produces desirable results.

Wade Cook, with his brilliant style, uses puts as a positive, or offensive, strategy. He achieves this by selling naked (or uncovered) puts. This strategy is used on stocks that have had some good news (positive earnings, stock split announcement, or trend reversal). Such good news usually results in an increase in the price of the stock. In such a case, Wade will sell puts with the expectation that the stock price will be driven higher than the strike price of the put, resulting in the put expiring worthless. Remember, when you sell an option, the cash hits your account the next day. Selling puts is, therefore, an extremely powerful strategy. You receive the cash now, and if the stock performs according to your expectations, you simply keep the cash.

On the other hand, if the stock takes a dip and is put to you, it is discounted by the cash previously received from selling the put. The strategy does have some drawbacks for the new or smaller investor. First of all, it is cash intensive because your broker will want to make sure you have the capability to purchase the stock if it is put to you. Theoretically, the stock could drop to zero and you would still have to buy the stock at the strike price. In addition, selling naked puts requires a higher level of option trading capability. Most brokers will usually not allow inexperienced traders to sell naked puts. However, this is a strategy that all serious traders should get qualified for in order to take advantage of the wonderful benefits this strategy provides. For example,

> **Risk varies inversely with knowledge.**
>
> *Irving Fuller*

on Friday, January 20th the trading department placed an order to sell puts on GATX Corporation (GMT) based on the news of a stock split announcement. The stock was trading around $73, and an order was placed to sell 10 contracts of the February $70 puts. The puts were bid at $1^7/16 x $1^5/8. The order was filled within the spread at $1^9/16. That means $1,562.50 (minus commissions) was placed in the account the next day. Let's take a look at what the requirements were to be able to do this trade. First, at some point, the account had to be approved for trading naked options. Then to do this trade, 30% of the strike price had to be held for margin. (Remember, when you sell an option you do not own, you take on an obligation, which must be covered.) Since it was the $70 strike, and 10 contracts, the amount of money necessary to do this trade is $70 x 1,000 x .3 = $21,000.

As you can see, even though there is a nice amount of money to be made in a short amount of time, it is the up-front requirements that prevent a lot of prospective and interest investors from using this strategy. Also, the risk of selling naked put options can be substantial (See WIN, Journal of Trades, Put Options).

There is an alternative to selling naked puts—one that provides the financial rewards of selling puts, the safety of a long position (owning a right rather than selling an obligation), and does not tie up nearly as much cash. Most importantly, virtually anyone that can write a covered call will be able to do this strategy. The first step in using this strategy successfully is to change your way of thinking about put options. Instead of thinking negatively about puts, start viewing them in a positive light. Since we are trading in a highly volatile market where the trend can be up or down at any given time, we need to have enough tools in our box to take care of whatever job we face. In other

> Things do not change; we change.
>
> *Henry David Thoreau*

words, we need to be able to play whatever hand the market deals us. If the stock we are playing shows a positive trend and we buy a call option, we have only one chance of being successful. The stock price must increase significantly. Only after it has done so will this trade be profitable. The purpose of this chapter is to introduce you to a strategy that gives you a greater chance of having a profitable trade. We are going to do this by giving ourselves alternative actions for when a stock does not perform the way we expect it to. We will use a strategy that does require some diligence (a necessary characteristic of *all* successful options traders) but allows you to put in place some "hooks" to protect your position.

> Learning is not attained by chance, it must be sought for with ardor and attended to with diligence.
>
> *Abigail Adams*

When trading options, we like to work with an underlying security that has a fair amount of volatility. That is, we like to use stocks that have a Beta of 1.3 or greater. (Refer to Wade Cook's book, *Stock Market Miracles* or WIN for more information on Beta). This high amount of "implied" volatility is what prompts the market makers to place premiums on the options that make them attractive to us as investors. As mentioned earlier, we want to use this strategy on a stock that has shown some movement. Attempting to use this on a relatively flat stock (RD, CCE) may not achieve the desired results. What we want to do is find a situation such as was the case with Citicorp (CCI) in December '97. As was the case with most stocks, CCI was affected by the October downturn and was battling back after showing signs of support at $115 (See Chart #1).

Chart #1

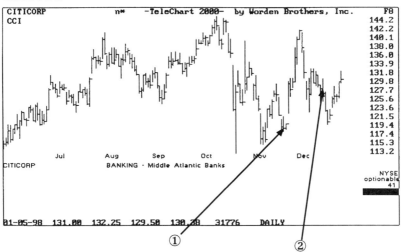

```
CITICORP          n*      -TeleChart 2000- by Worden Brothers, Inc.    F8
CCI                                                                    144.2
                                                                       142.2
                                                                       140.1
                                                                       138.0
                                                                       136.0
                                                                       133.9
                                                                       131.8
                                                                       129.8
                                                                       127.7
                                                                       125.6
                                                                       123.6
                                                                       121.5
                                                                       119.4
                                                                       117.4
                                                                       115.3
        Jul       Aug     Sep      Oct      Nov      Dec               113.2
CITICORP          BANKING · Middle Atlantic Banks
                                                                      NYSE
                                                                   optionable
                                                                       41

01-05-98  131.00  132.25  129.50  130.30   31776    DAILY
                        ①                         ②
```

Referring to the chart, observe that on November 25th, the stock opened at $120, had a high of $120^{15}/16$, a low of $117 ^{1}/2$, and closed at $119^{1}/4$ (see arrow #①). At this point, the stock is in a definite downward trend. But the main questions we need to ask at this point are: Will this trend continue, and for how long? Do we buy a call? De we buy a put, and if so, at what strike price? When these types of questions arise, I have been buying a closest strike price put. Here is my logic for doing. Considering the recent volatility, compared to the longer term rising trend, might a long term call be warranted? In this case, I felt that the best investment would be to buy the December $120 put. By doing this, I effectively double my chances of winning on this particular trade. First, if the stock continues its downward trend, I would hold the put as a long position and then sell it for a profit. (Don't forget, when we buy an option, we have the right, not the obligation, to do something.) Now, if the stock reverses its downward trend and

> The actions of men are like the index of a book ... they point out what is most remarkable in them.
>
> *Heinrich Heine*

instead becomes bullish (and this is where the diligence and the beauty of the strategy comes in) I will sell the December $125 put. Remember, I first bought the December $120 put, and have now sold the next higher strike price put. What I have done is to create a Bull Put Spread (sometimes called a Put Credit Spread) one leg at a time. Here is the scenario:

Bought:　　　　　December $120 put at $1.50

Sold:　　　　　　December $125 put at $3.125

I created a $5 spread ($125-$120), and put $1⅝ in my account! Here is how it works: I bought the December $120 put for just $1.50 (and this money is removed *from* my account the next day). I sold the December $125 put for $3.125 (and this money is placed *in* my account the next day). The difference between the two transactions is $1⅝ ($3.125 - $1.50 = $1⅝). Remember, we place the emphasis on selling instead of buying!

Here is how this Bull Put Spread will play out:

1.　If the stock stays above $125 at expiration, no one would want to put their stock to me at that price, since they could sell it on the open market for a higher price. Therefore, I get to keep the credit of $1⅝. Since I did this 10 times, that was $1,625 (i.e., when setting up a spread, you tell the broker how many contracts you want to buy or sell). When creating a spread like this, it is important to understand the potential risk. You have created a $5 spread (the most you can lose is $5). However, the credit for creating this spread is $1⅝. Thus your exposure here is the $5 spread minus the credit you received for creating it ($5 - $1⅝ = $3⅜). Since this credit

> In skating over thin ice, our safety is in our speed.
>
> *Ralph Waldo Emerson*

spread was done 10 times, the amount held in the account was $5,000 - $1,625 = $3,387.50. The reason is that although this is a covered put, since a part of it was sold (the December $125 put) without owning it, an amount has to be held in your account to cover the liability. You can compare this to the amount held for margin when selling a naked put. And in this instance, at expirations the stock was above $125 (see arrow #②).

2. So what happens if the stock is not above $125 at expiration? As long as the stock is below $125 there is a chance that the stock could be put to you. (Remember, when you sell an option you have an obligation.) If this happens you might want to consider unwinding this position— that is, buying back the upper leg. Also, if the stock continues downward, this becomes a second opportunity to make a profit. By holding onto the long position (your right to put the stock to someone at $120), if the stock price continues down, the corresponding increase in the option price often makes up for the cost of buying back the short position (your obligation to buy the stock at $125).

> **Money is like an arm or a leg—use it or lose it.**
>
> *Henry Ford*

This was the case with Iomega (IOM) at the end of November. The company was rumored to be a takeover candidate, so the stock had been a nice upward range rider (see Chart #2). The critical question was whether this trend could be sustained. On November 25th, when the stock was $27^1/2, the December $25 put was purchased for $2^1/2 (see arrow #①). If the stock price increase as expected, the December $30 put would be sold, thereby completing the Bull Put Spread. The stock did climb up to $29 and the December $30 put was sold for $4 (see arrow #②). The result was a net credit of $1^1/2 ($4 - $2^1/2). The stock reached a high of $33^1/2 and the outlook was fairly bright. As is often the case in the stock market, looks can be deceiving. The stock abruptly turned around and began a near free-fall (see arrow #③). Not to worry—this is where the powerful side of this strategy comes in. If a call option had been purchased, this turnaround in the stock could have spelled disaster. But the wonderful thing about a put credit spread is, as the stock started its slide—and this is where the diligence commissions in—and moved towards $30, one should consider unwinding the position by buying back the short leg (the December $30 put). This was done at a cost of $5³/4 ($1 ³/4 more than it had been sold for).

Since all indications were that the stock was going to continue to slide, the upper leg was bought back and the December $25 was left in place to gain in value and hopefully sell at a profit. Sure enough, the stock did lose value and a GTC (Good Till Canceled) order was placed to sell the option when the stock reached $24¹/2. This order was filled and the option was sold for $7³/8. The bottom line for this deal is that there was a net profit of $1¹/8. This is pretty cool stuff for what otherwise would have been a losing position.

Chart #2

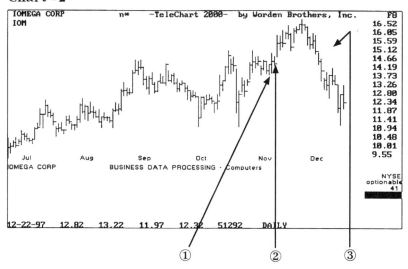

This strategy has been used on Dell Computer (DELL). Dell is a volatile stock, where using a spread to cover your position can save you a lot of grief (see Chart #3). In November, Dell hit a post-split low of $70 (see arrow #①). It then ran up to $87.25 where it encountered resistance (see arrow #②). Dell then dipped down to $75.25 (see arrow #③). At this point, I was unsure of which way the stock would head, so I purchased the December $75 put for $2¹/₈. Once again the scenario shows that, if the stock continues downward, the put will be sold at a profit. If the stock goes up, then the next higher strike price put will be sold. (Notice the emphasis on selling!) When the stock reached $79 the December $80 put was sold for $3¹/₂ (see arrow #④). This created a net credit of $1³/₈. Dell then ran up, pulled back, and on expiration closed at $80³/₄. At this price there is a slight chance that the stock would be put to me, however that did not happen. This brings us to the case of what happens if the stock gets put to you.

Chart #3

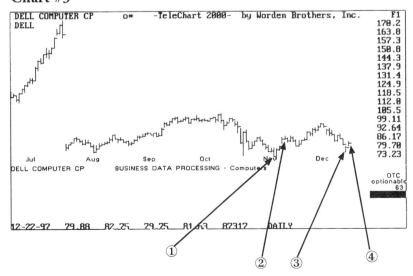

This happened with VLSI Technology (VLSI-see Chart #4). In early December the stock was slammed down to $18^7/8 (see arrow #①). When the stock bounced back and reached $21^1/2, the December $22^1/2 put was purchased for $1^3/4 (see arrow #②). The stock turned around and when it reached $22, the December $22^1/2 put was sold for $2^3/4 (see arrown #③). The stock then went on a downward move and at expirations, closed at $19^9/16 (see arrow #④). Needless to say, I was in a position to have some stock put to me. If this would have been a naked put, I would have had to do some fancy footwork if I did not want to own this stock. But, once again, here is where the beauty of doing the put spread comes in. With the stock being $3+ in the money at expiration, it was a sure thing that someone would exercise the December $22^1/2 put. When that happened, the position was covered by exercising the December $20 put. This is something your broker should do without your having to tell them, but to be on the safe side, tell your broker you want to do a "same day substitution" (SDS). This gives you the opportunity to sell stock that you might not necessarily want to own. (Remember, when you sell a naked put, you do that because you don't mind owning the stock at that price. That is not one of the obligations with this strategy.)

Chart #4

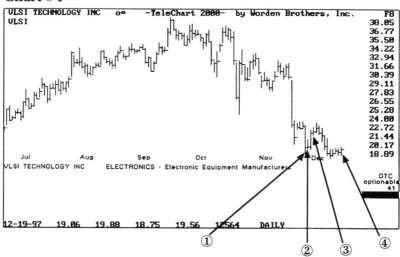

The bottom line for this position at expiration was that the December $22^1/2$ put was assigned to me at a cost of $12,537 (five contracts). I then assigned five contracts of the December $20 puts for $11,212.62 for a net loss of $1,324.38. This represents a significant reduction in what could have been lost if this had just been done as a call option or as a naked put. This is another one of the strong points about this strategy, being able to limit your downside. Some might say, "Well, this also limits your upside." This is a true statement, but if we are using the Meter Drop strategy (cash to asset to cash), we are not looking for the "big score." We are just getting into trades for a few weeks or less (basically the same amount of time you would be in a covered call play) and taking a nice return, with limited risk.

> The money is in the "Meter Drop."
>
> *Wade Cook*

Let's review some of the salient points for this strategy:

First, even if you are an experienced trader, I strongly encourage you to paper trade (Simutrade) this strategy to get a good feel for it. Find a stock that has some good volatility. Look for good news, range riders, strong growth, new highs, new lows. Be fairly bullish on the stock. Remember, the optimum position is to sell the next strike price above. Buy the bottom leg when the stock is near a strike price. Don't forget, there is an amount held back for covering the spread. (Amount of spread minus the credit received. Brokers have no sense of humor when it comes to House or Fed calls.)

Sell the next strike above when there is $1^1/4$ or more for the credit (usually two to four weeks out). Try to sell the upper leg before a holiday. Market makers tend to reduce any time value in a premium over a holiday.

Pay attention!!! This is still an option trade and diligence is due.

If the stock price goes below the upper strike price, do not panic if you are more than a week away from expiration. Remember only 20% of all option contracts are exercised, and the majority of these are done on expiration. Check charts and especially news. If it is just a temporary dip in the stock, it's not a problem. If it is a prolonged decline, look into buying back the upper leg when the stock price goes to a dollar or two in the money. If you wait for the stock price to go any deeper in the money, it could be prohibitively expensive to buy back the short position. If you miss the buyback point and get assigned, you have the choice of taking the stock or exercising the long position and assigning the stock put to you (same day substitution).

> Investing is reporting. I told him to imagine he had been assigned an in-depth article about his own paper. He'd ask a lot of questions and dig up a lot of facts. He'd know The Washington Post. And that's all there is to it.
>
> *Warren Buffett*

Be aware! Puts have a tendency to move at a faster rate (higher delta) than call options.

Above all, have fun with this strategy. The purpose of being in the stock market is to make a better life for you and your family. Don't stray from rules, find stocks that file the strategy, and don't massage the strategy to fit the stock. Follow the formulas. Make sure you have good timely information (WIN, your broker) and use it well.

About The Author

ich Simmons was born and raised in the Midwest. During his school years, he was actively involved in sports and public speaking. Among his achievements are Top Speaker at the Forensic club at his high school. He was very active in the church where many times he gave the Sunday sermon as a junior minister. After attending Coe College, he embarked on a varied career, which eventually brought him to the Pacific Northwest. There he pursued a career in the high-tech industry.

At the strong urging of his wife, he attended a Wade Cook seminar, where he then started following the strategies taught to him by Mr. Cook. After giving a testimonial at a Wade Cook function, he was asked to join the Wade Cook team. He started in the sales department, then moved on to the seminars, where, as a result of his electronics background, was asked to perform the technical duties at the Wall Street Workshops. From there, he became a lead Wall Street Workshop speaker.

He is now semi-retired, trading the market and being a guest speaker at the Wall Street Workshop. He lives in Covington, Washington with Sally, his wife of 15 years.

Success Through DUCks

Keven Hart

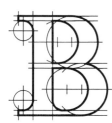

uy low . . . sell high; the first rule of investing in the stock market. To paraphrase Will Rogers, "Don't gamble with your money. Buy a nice stock that's going to go up and sell it when it gets high."

His tongue-in-cheek humor is actually great advice, but how do you tell which stocks are going to go up, when to buy, and when to sell? As I have invested in the stock market, I have learned some valuable lessons that play to this question. I wish Will were still alive so I could share with him what I have discovered.

> A study of economics usually reveals that the best time to buy anything is usually last year.
>
> *Marty Allen*

The first lesson has to do with which stocks are going to go up. I learned this one from my friend Wade Cook. Wade, myself, and a third friend, Joel Black had formed a corporation dedicated to youth work and excellence training. In the course of working with Wade and his financial organization, I saw him using some unique stock market strategies and asked him if I could sit in on his Wall Street Workshop program to learn some things. What I saw nearly knocked my socks off. He was using option-based trading to earn extraordinary returns. There was too much in that workshop to even try and cover here, but here is the portion that pertains to stocks going up.

I discovered that companies which announce stock splits have a marked tendency to rise again toward their pre-split price. When I say marked, I mean that if you bought 10 stock split companies and played them, you would come out ahead eight or nine times out of ten using the system Wade had developed. That creates good enough odds that even if you knew nothing other than how to call your broker to place a trade, you could do very well indeed in the market. (I have since verified through experience what Wade taught me. I have also reviewed studies which came to the same conclusion.) Now I had in hand the answer to the first part of the question I posed at the beginning of this discussion, namely, how to choose companies that are going up.

> If you don't invest very much, then defeat doesn't hurt very much and winning is not very exciting.
>
> *Dick Vermeil*

I found the next answer before I even asked the question. I had assumed that one should stay away from option trading because it carried significantly more risk than stock trades. (Remember, an option, specifically a call option, is the right to purchase stock away from its owner at a set price, on or before a set date at which time the option expires. People generally purchase call options in the hope that the stock will run up in price. They can then exercise the option to buy the stock at the lower, predetermined price and resell it at the current price, which is higher, and take the profit.) What I have learned is that options are viewed as risky only because of some numbers that are commonly quoted by brokers to "protect" their clients. Those numbers say that only 20% of all options purchased are ever exercised. The statement is true, but it only tells part of the story.

Most options players are gambling that a stock will go up based on a hunch, or a hope, or some sort of news that generally plays out in short order. They are then left holding an option on a stock that either does not rise to the point they want, or backs off before they make the choice to exercise their option and purchase the stock at the lower price the call option entitled them to. These traders have two strikes against them: First, they are betting on a stock without much to substantiate the choice and second, most of the time such traders forget that they are paying for time and that time will eventually run out. Most watch the stock move up only a little, if any. Then many of them see the stock pull back down in price and end up holding their option until it expires, hoping all the while the stock will move back up. Instead of recouping some of the investment by selling their option at a loss before it expires, they wring their hands until the expiration date, and then go back to scrutinize their formula for choosing a company to play options on.

Most of them miss the real power in options which is this: when there is a movement in the stock, there is a magnified movement in the option. If the stock moves up, the call option rises too, but the percent of increase is much higher in the option than it is in the stock.

> Now is always the most difficult time to invest.
>
> *Anonymous*

That brings us to the second question and the central topic of this discussion. If stock-split companies are the ones to concentrate on, how and when do you buy and sell?

How

The way to use call options is to go back to the "Will Rogers" theory of investing in options: only invest in companies that are going to go up, like stock-split companies. That's the formula adjustment that you and I as options players need to make. Then we need to get good at getting out, not by exercising the option, but by reselling it. The question I hadn't asked yet was, "How do I supercharge my investments?" The answer: "Trade the options, not the stock."

If call options increase when the underlying stock moves up, and stock split companies display a marked tendency to do just that, let's buy call options on stock split companies and resell them at an acceptable profit. The net effect is that you get a bigger bang for your buck. (For an in-depth explanation of the stock/option price relationship see Wade Cook's *Wall Street Money Machine*.)

I play stock split companies by buying options on the company and reselling them for a profit as the stock (and therefore the option) rises in value. That way I get the maximum effect from the stock's increase in value. That's the "how."

When

Many times I will buy options as soon as the split announcement is made. To do this you need a good broker who is trained to call you as soon as the announcement comes across the news wire. Generally I do this on issues that are small, exciting, and volatile. When such companies make the announcement of a stock split, there is usually an immediate run up in the stock price, carrying the call option price higher.

Remember that time is money.

Benjamin Franklin

I also buy call options just before or just after the stock splits because there is often a lesser run up at those two points in time. There are certain factors that play into that trade which I find useful, but won't take the time to explain here because I have one other play which I like more than all others combined. Across the next several months as the stock moves to and through the split, there are several opportunities to play rises in the price with call options. Generally these splits take place within a month or two and the stocks remain playable for several months after the split. Sometimes they stay in play for a year or more. They are playable as long as they move back toward their old price range. They may even move up and split again.

DUCk hunting

My favorite strategy for playing options on stock split companies is to hunt for a specific play I call a DUCk. This is an acronym for "Dipping Undervalued Call." The stock market makes up weird terms like LEAPS® and DRIPS to convey meaning without lengthy explanation. I'll take the same liberty here. Now, here is the background for this type of play.

A company we will call XYZ is doing very well; they have a good market share or maybe they are the leader in their industry. They have rising revenues, rising book value, and rising earnings. The stock is currently trading at $100. They have every reason to suppose that, if they split the shares 2:1, investors will see it as an opportunity to buy a company that is on the move at half the price ($50), and the stock will eventually move back to its current range and be worth twice as much. That is a simplified explanation. You can bet that the board is not doing the split to make it easier on the potential investor. They want to be worth more by increasing the valuation of the company. It's that simple. If they are right, and most of the time they are, it creates a great opportunity for options players like us.

Concurrent with the split announcement, many such companies will announce an increase in dividends which attracts more investor interest and enhances the upward movement of the stock after the announcement. As the stock moves upward, many stockholders see it as an opportunity to sell at a profit. The taking of profits often creates a temporary dip in the stock price and therefore (I hope you are running ahead of me here) a drop in the price of the option. If the stock has demonstrated well defined upward momentum, we can go in, buy calls, and ride the demonstrated strength of the stock toward the split date. As long as

> Take care to sell your horse before he dies. The art of life is passing losses on.
>
> *Robert Frost*

the fundamentals of the company don't change, the same basics which drove the stock to its high point before will drive it there again. It may take several years, or it may take only take a few months.

Now we get to see the real strength of this strategy. If you buy a call three months out so you can ride past the two or three areas where these stocks have a tendency to run up and hold those calls through to a point where you are nearing expiration date, you not only start to see your option begin to decay as you run down on time, but you have missed some opportunities along the way. That may sound strange since you have held the call across the entire time, so let me explain.

The path from the point where the company announces to where it actually splits is not a straight angle upward. The stock will usually run up, pull back some, run up again and perhaps run several times through this scenario before the split, and several more after the split. Whenever it pulls back, it covers the ground it lost again as it moves back up. If you can time your entrances and exits well, you can make the same money twice as you cover the same ground again. For instance, if a stock is trading at $45 and pulls back to $40, you can buy call options, ride the rise in the stock upward, get out as the stock reaches a point where it lost momentum before, sell the call at perhaps the $50 mark, then wait for the call to complete its pullback before buying calls again for another ride up. If you buy back in at $45 you would be covering the ground between $45 and $50 twice. If you buy options one time and sell only once, you miss all those extra gains as the stock dances upward. You also see good gains in the price of your option go out the window each time it does a pullback. Eventually, as the time value comes out of your option, you find that your gains have been minimized.

> The road up and the road down is one and the same.
>
> *Heraclitus*

You can identify a DUCk by watching the charts of stock split companies and looking for a 5 to 10% pullback in the price of the stock between the time the company announces the split and the time the split actually takes place. The situation is that you have a company that is doing well and its fundamentals will drive the price on up after a pullback occurs. The classic play lies between the announcement and the split. The split is the best of all types of news and will usually draw the price of the stock upward like a magnet. The fact that the split has passed does not eliminate the stock from this type of play as it did with Ascend Communications, for instance. This stock split twice inside one year and was moving toward a theoretical third split at this writing. As long as the basic circumstances surrounding a stock split company have not changed it is not unreasonable to assume that it will continue to move upward.

In a classic DUCk play the stock moves regularly and is easy to follow. You simply let the stock turn the corner on its run/pullback cycle and either buy or sell your option as indicated by the turn. I know it sounds simplistic, but it is not a complicated strategy. "Buy low, sell high" is about as simple as it gets.

There are several items to keep in mind. It's always a good idea to make sure the stock has turned the corner. If the stock has a history of sharp turns, assume such is the case. See what it has done in the past. I don't think we want to complicate the strategy by second guessing history.

> **If I had my life to live over again, I'd make the same mistakes, only sooner.**
>
> *Tallulah Bankhead*

It's usually a good idea to match a short-term option (three months out or less) with a longer term option (four months out or longer) in case the stock does turn south for an extended period of time.

It does happen. Buying extra time by going farther out for the expiration date may give a stock which has taken an unexpected hit, the time it needs to recover and move your options back in the black.

> **There is only one success—to be able to spend your life in your own way.**
>
> *Christopher Morley*

Take more time to spend with your family. I know that doesn't affect this stock play, but it will remind you why you are doing this in the first place.

I use DUCks as my primary options play. They have been so dependable for me that I go back to the old saying, "If it looks like a DUCk, quacks like a DUCk, and walks like a DUCk, it's probably a DUCk."

Happy hunting.

◆ ◆ ◆

This chapter contains excerpts from Keven Hart's special report series published by Lighthouse Publishing Group, Inc. For more information on this series call 1-800-872-7411.

About The Author

even Hart is a self-proclaimed "farm-kid" who uses a common sense approach to both business and life. "Make money and do good things with it." "Take an aggressive strategy and practice it conservatively." Balance is a key ingredient in his philosophy and his action.

Holding a masters degree emphasizing experiential education, he tends to "find what works and build on it." Mr. Hart currently serves as CEO of HLS Corporation, a provider of research and instruction in stock market strategies and he is an active trader and investor. He and his brother, Dr. Richard K. Hart, instruct a series of workshops on the subject of trading at home professionally.

In addition to his authorship of this current work, he has authored or co-authored three other works: *Cash Crop, Home Grown,* and *Patterns: The Challenge of Change.* He and his sweetheart of 20 plus years, Debbie, and reside on a horse farm in the Washington Cascades because, as he says, "Hay is a lot cheaper than drug rehabilitation."

Planning For Success

JJ Childers

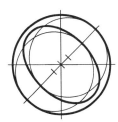

O ne of the greatest desires of individuals today is to make more money. However, many times we get so caught up in worrying about how we can make more money that we never take the time to learn how to keep it. Wade Cook, in his books and seminars, often points to the fact that most people spend more time planning their vacations than they spend planning their financial futures. It's alarming, but true, that there are more 18 year olds in this country who can afford to write a $500 check than there are 65 year olds. How could this possibly be? Basically, it's because the vast majority of individuals in our country never take the time to learn to keep more of what they earn.

> **Businesses planned for service are apt to succeed; businesses planned for profit are apt to fail.**
>
> *Nicholas M. Butler*

Many of our problems can be solved if we concentrate on three key areas. These three areas are: 1) asset protection, 2) estate planning, and 3) tax reduction. These topics are so important to the overall success of individuals that they need to be addressed one by one.

First, the area of asset protection has become increasingly important over the past several decades due to the substantial rise in the number of lawsuits filed in this country. We've all heard or read about some of the truly unbelievable lawsuits that have been filed (successfully) over the last few years. All one needs to do is turn on their television set or flip through the newspaper and you see a new lawsuit which has been filed. Shockingly, when you flip on the television set or read through the newspaper awhile the down the road, it turns out that these lawsuits were either settled or won by the plaintiffs. With the size of many of these judgments (including punitive damages), perhaps the most surprising thing is that there aren't *more* lawsuits filed (if that's possible!).

> If a man dies and leaves his estate in an uncertain condition, the lawyers become his heirs.
>
> *Ed Howe*

Asset protection is an area which is often overlooked because people seem to believe that lawsuits are something that may happen to everyone else, but not to them. The odds of your being a target of one of these lawsuits has never been greater. Hence, the need for asset protection has never been greater. In order to protect your assets, you must have a plan! There are definite ways to increase your protection, but you must implement these strategies before it's too late.

The second key area which you must concentrate on is the area of estate planning. For years, estate planning was viewed as an area only for the "truly" wealthy. If your last name wasn't Carnegie, Mellon, Rockefeller, or Kennedy, you need not worry about estate planning. Is that the case today? Not at all. Today, everyone needs to be concerned about estate planning because of a process known as probate. The probate process is a system set up by the government to provide for the orderly distribution of your estate upon your death. As with all good government programs, probate has many steps involved which make it a very time consuming and a very costly process. One sure

way of reducing the time and money involved in the probate process is by avoiding probate all together. In order to avoid
that process, however, you must have a plan!

The greater thing in this world is not so much where we stand as in what direction we are going.

Oliver Wendell Holmes

Through the use of various entities and
strategies, you can avoid probate as well as
substantially reduce the amount of your taxable estate. After all, what
is the point of spending year after year of your entire life working to
build up and accumulate a nice amount of wealth only to lose half of
it to the government and to fees? Estate planning is about preserving
more of what you've accumulated so that it can be passed down to
those who mean the most to you-your family, your church, and chari-
ties. You must take advantage of planning procedures.

Our third key area is the one which generates the most interest,
by far. That is the area of tax reduction. It seems that no matter where
I go, whether I'm teaching seminars, talking which clients, flying on
airplanes, or even at church, everyone wants to talk to me about how
disgusted they are with their tax situation. I always ask these people
the same question: "What are you doing about it?" I truly want to
know what these people plan to do in order to reduce their tax bill.
The answer I usually get is, "Well, I'm … uh … I'm complaining
about it!" Is that enough? Will that really accomplish anything? The
people who I'm really impressed with are those individuals who are
willing to do something about it, those individuals who are willing to
spend their time and money doing what it takes to reduce their tax
bills. I see these people who are serious enough about reducing their
tax bill that they are willing to take time out of their schedules, time
off from work to attend my seminars. These are the people who will
be successful in their efforts to pay less in taxes, because these are the

people who are willing to do something about it. By taking the time to read this book, you are demonstrating that you are willing to do something about your tax situation and I commend you on that!

This is an overall process which you must go through however. The simple fact is: you have to *learn* to reduce your tax bill! If you don't believe that then you need to ask yourself some questions. When was the last time you received a letter from the IRS telling you that you failed to take all of the potential deductions which may applied to you? Have you received such a letter? Do you expect to? Don't hold your breath! *You* are the only one who can do something about your tax bill. You are in control. But you must be willing to do what it takes. You must have a plan.

> **There is nothing sinister in so arranging one's affairs as to keep taxes as low as possible.**
>
> *Judge Learned Hand*

Now that we've established the fact that you must have a plan which addresses these three key areas, we find ourselves in a new situation. We must now determine the best way to design our plan. In designing this plan, we must apply a three step process which should be applied in all areas of our lives when it comes to decision making. That three step process is as follows: 1) gather information, 2) analyze the information, and 3) implement and take action. This process is so important to your success that we need to spend some time working through it. Additionally, it just so happens that the failure to adopt this process (#3 in particular) is why most people find themselves in an undesirable situation, why they pay too much in taxes or are saddled with lawsuits.

The first step is to gather information. Whether it be gathering information on investments, strategies to pursue, or which entity to establish, you must first gather the pertinent information. This is crucial because the more information you have, the better the chances of a good decision being made. I must offer a brief caveat here, however. Do not get bogged down on getting every bit of information. Many times, you will not need every bit of information in order to make an informed decision. I often ask people who make a lot of money in the stock market whether they had every imaginable piece of information before they made the trade. The response I almost always get is that they laugh and say, "Of course not." The point is, these people got enough information to make an informed decision and then moved to the next step. Do not fool yourself into thinking that you are right on track simply because you gather information. While this is a crucial step, it is of absolutely no value to you unless you take that information and *apply* it to the next step.

> If a man write a better book, preach a better sermon, or make a better mousetrap than his neighbor, though he build his house in the woods, the world will make a beaten path to his door.
>
> *Ralph Waldo Emerson*

That next step is to analyze the information. Information alone is of no use to you until you analyze it. Through the analysis of information, you are able to come to conclusions. You are able to determine if the information is worthwhile, valuable information. If the information turns out to be valuable, you can then take that information in the next step of process. Once again, you must fight the urge to simply stop in the analysis stage. This is perhaps the biggest obstacle which one must overcome. It is what's known as "the paralysis of analysis." It occurs when you get so caught up on the analysis of the information that you become paralyzed. You simply do nothing. Is it very easy to simply do nothing? Absolutely! That's the easiest thing of all. That is the one sure way to guarantee your outcome.

While it's true that you know you can't fail if you do nothing, it's also painfully true that you know for sure that you won't succeed! If you do nothing, what do you get? Nothing!

All three steps of this process are critical, but the third step is by far the most important. That is the step of acting on the information which you've gathered and analyzed. Without implementing the information, you cannot take advantage of the benefits offered. For our purposes, if you truly desire to protect your assets, plan your estate, and reduce your tax bill. You cannot accomplish these goals unless you establish and implement the entities which provide for these advantages. You could have all of the information contained in the treatises, law books, and tax code completely memorized and understood better than any other professional, but if you do not act on

> **Knowing is not enough; we must apply. Willing is not enough; we must do.**
>
> *Johann Wolfgang von Goethe*

that knowledge, it will not benefit you. The most important step in anything is *action*! For our purposes, the required action is to establish an entity structuring plan.

When evaluating the type of plan that will best fit your situation, you have a wide variety of options out there. Where should you go? What is the best type of entity to implement? What type of plan will be best for accomplishing our three goals of asset protection, estate planning and tax reduction? Well, I will have to give you my "attorney" answer to that question. My attorney answer is: it depends! How's that? (Spoken like a true attorney.) Actually, it really does depend upon your particular needs. An overall entity structuring plan is like a suit. Quite obviously, we can't all wear the exact same suit. We each need a suit which will best fit our particular dimensions, our particular needs. This significantly narrows the road which we may take toward establishing our plan.

If we are looking for a narrowly tailored plan which will best suit our particular needs, we can immediately weed out certain entity sources. Without actually commenting on these particular sources, I will show you a process to go through. In evaluating a potential source of your entity structuring, ask yourself whether the plan you will receive will be tailored to your needs. You can be the judge of that. If you buy an entity kit to do it yourself, are you receiving the best professional review? If you proceed to incorporate "in as little as eight minutes for as little as $45," are you getting the type of specialized attention you're looking for? You get what you pay for.

At the other end of the spectrum is the type of plan which is narrowly tailored to fit your needs yet requires expensive payments for that plan to be explained. I've encountered situations where clients are literally afraid to ask questions of their attorneys about their entity plans for fear of being billed. Too many times, those clients will never fully understand how entity structuring works and never comprehend how their affairs are structured. When clients themselves do not understand, imagine the frustrations encountered by the families of these individuals upon their deaths. They have no idea what to do in such a situation. One great way of having these concerns addressed is by keeping accurate and dependable records of all necessary information.

> **Your own mind is a sacred enclosure into which nothing harmful can enter except by your permission.**
>
> *Ralph Waldo Emerson*

When establishing your plan, it is crucial that you work with a company that can give you the best of both worlds. You need to have a narrowly tailored plan which you understand and which you are able to build upon your understanding at minimal cost. The only company which I am familiar with which offers this incredible package is Wade Cook Seminars, the company with which I am affiliated.

This is the reason for my affiliation. I honestly believe, as I'm sure you will find, that this company will be able to accommodate any and all needs you may have with your entity structuring. But you must make the call.

In deciding what type of plan will best suit your individual situation, you will encounter various entities. Which entity will be the best for you remains to be determined. However, I firmly believe that the entity structuring process is one of the quintessential ingredients in your quest for success. Now, more than at any time in the history of our country, you must have these entities implemented into your affairs. **You must have a plan!**

> **It wasn't raining when Noah built the ark.**
>
> *Howard Ruff*

◆ ◆ ◆

This chapter contains excerpts from JJ Childers' book, *The Secret Millionaire*, published by Lighthouse Publishing Group, Inc. This book will be available soon in better bookstores.

About the author

ohn V. Childers, Jr., also know as JJ Childers, is a licensed attorney specializing in the areas of asset protection, estate planning, and tax reduction. His unique background provides a fresh no-nonsense look into the world of legal entities. He gained a valuable working knowledge of how laws are developed through his experience as a clerk in the state legislature's House of Representatives. While working in the office of the attorney general, he was able to see firsthand how government agencies operate.

Through his experience as an intern clerk for a federal appeals court judge, he acquired an important insight into the judicial process. Additionally, his work for a private plaintiff's law firm taught him the importance of a good asset protection plan. Combining this experience with the background of growing up in the entrepreneurial field of real estate investment and development, he offers an approach to legal entities which is badly needed in today's litigious society. He currently spends his time speaking with groups throughout the country on the importance of preserving wealth and protecting assets through innovative entity structuring.

How Ya Gonna Succeed, Jack?

Wade Cook

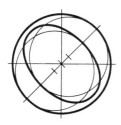

nce I discussed success with a successful sales representative. He said that everyone knows how to be a success but just won't do it. I disagreed somewhat, but I pressed on. To me, very few successful people or companies had a game plan, and if they did in the beginning, they were not currently doing what they originally set out to do. Facts from other collected data bear this out. Many inventions, or discoveries, things we use and take for granted (penicillin, laser discoveries, global positioning systems) are the by-products of other technologies—and some stumbled on by complete accident. Lucky for us someone was astute enough to see the possibilities.

> It isn't that they can't see the solution. It is that they can't see the problem.
>
> *G. K. Chesterton*

He was not swayed. He firmly believed when I finished that "not doing it" was sine qua non to failure. I can't disagree totally, because even if people know how to do it, or what to do to make it, most don't. Now, by writing the word "most" in the last sentence it may seem that many people or "most" people know how. I say very, very few people know how to be truly successful. And of the few that know how, only a handful are truly happy when it happens. But happiness is a discussion we'll deal with in other works.

> To avoid criticism, do nothing, say nothing, be nothing.
>
> *Elbert Hubbard*

Also, I want to clear up a misconception that may occur if the reader thinks that what I wrote a few paragraphs ago about companies and people changing or not doing what they set out to do, means that I don't like change, creativity, or innovation.

If a person needs a detailed plan about what we're trying to accomplish, how we're going to make, promote, and distribute widgets, a plan to be successful or to get started on the road, then great. If it doesn't work, adapt, change, modify, innovate, and push on. Success and development of personal traits is important to me. One of the things I teach at our Wall Street Workshop is to bet on the jockey, not on the horse. I like success even if it comes after several setbacks. Get started and make changes along the way. It's called "production towards perfection." As my good friend Robert Hondel says, "Let Serendipity take care of it."

Bootstraps—high high bonuses

Back to my discussion with my friend. I told him that at my financial seminars we give specific formulas for making money. These formulas, methods, and techniques are well defined, easy to understand and easier to implement. They are time tested. I ask people who tell me that at the two day event they made back the tuition and were ahead $6,400, or $8,200, or $1,400, what specific formula they used. They can explain it in detail. They bought the stock at $14.25 (rule one for covered call writing: buy in the $5 to $25 range), they bought on margin (rule two: only half the money is needed); they waited for the stock to rise to $15 or $16 (rule three: buy stocks which are volatile and roll or trade in a certain range), and then sell the $17.50 call the next month out (another short trade technique) and capture the $1.50 ($1,500 cash if ten contracts were sold) thereby getting a 20 to 40% one month gain (40% or even 60%) if called out (sell the stock).

They are happy as can be. They learned the formulas and the rules well. They experienced success and most importantly, they can repeat the process. If, as I've said so many times, one key to success is duplication and repetition, then they are well on their way.

Conversely, once in awhile, I talk to someone who loses money on a trade. These stories are so few and far between that I really don't know how to handle them. I emphasize, we never promised 100% successful trades. We don't make recommendations.

> We learn wisdom from failure much more than from success; we often discover what we will do by finding out what we will not do; and probably he who never made a mistake never made a discovery.
>
> *Samuel Smiles*

Here's how it goes. "What strategy did you use?" "I was doing an option on a stock split." "Okay, what was your plan?" "Just to make money." "Now specifically, which of the five times to do options on stock splits were you doing? Did you check the charts and the fundamentals? What was your exit point?" (I'm really big into "know your exit before you go in the entrance.") "Uh, uh, I don't know."

You see, that's not what we teach at the event. It's not what we do. If the person said this, "I bought the June 55C (call option) on XYZ for $2^3/8$. I was planning on a $2 to $3 jump in the stock the day or two before, on the split or exdividend date. That would push the option to $3^3/8$ and I'd get out at $1 profit ($500 or $1,000 or $10,000—depending on the quantity of contracts)." This strategy follows our model. If it doesn't perform as expected, learn from it and get on. You know I never get an answer like this. Losing comes from not following the rules, or a weird drop in the stock or market.

Now, some of you just estimated that at $2^3/8$, $2,375 would be lost—either partially or in total if the play doesn't work. Maybe you

> Even if you're on the right track, you'll get run over if you just sit there.
>
> *Will Rogers*

can't afford to lose that much. Okay, so let me tell you about Beth Anne. She came to the WSWS (Wall Street Workshop) and lost $2,980. She was devastated. Her husband was not happy. I read her letter, a chronology of trades, four total trades made at the WSWS. The day after the class the market dropped 120 points. Her particular option did not have enough time to recover. She actually started with $3,700 and lost $2,980. That's sad.

I asked her, "Did not the instructor explain to you diversification? Did he not use the examples of $5,000—if you have $5,000 to get started only $500 or $1,000 should be in options" (and only then if this is risk money, or money you don't need)? "Did he not explain how risky options are?" (Yes, they are great money makers but they have a downside risk.)

She answered, "Yes, yes, yes," to all of these questions. She blew it. She did not follow the most fundamental rules. She jumped in, but should have a) diversified, b) only used risk capital, c) gained more experience by paper trading, or doing one trade at a time to gain experience.

Many years ago I bought a restaurant. The previous owner told me that if the recipe for chowder called for a tablespoon of salt, the hardest thing he did was to get an employee to put in an exact tablespoon of salt. Not a palmful, not a heaping spoonful, not a guesstimate, but an exact tablespoon full.

I agree, getting our students to follow exact directions is often as difficult.

Just having knowledge is not a guarantee of success. Many doctors know how harmful smoking is but smoke anyway. Success and happiness come from the proper application of knowledge. Some call this wisdom.

Summary

Learn the formulas (rules) that you must follow to be successful.

Set a course.

Define as many obstacles as possible and how you'll solve problems. In fact, you'll be way ahead in life if you figure out what kind of problems you like to solve, or work on, and then get into that business.

Get up your resolve. List clearly what you have to do, are willing to do, and decide who needs to do it.

Get on with it. Life is not complicated. Yes, you have to do it, but you have to know what to do and get good at learning the formulas (methods, techniques).

Plan your work and work your plan.

Anonymous

◆ ◆ ◆

This chapter contains excerpts from Wade Cook's book, *Don't Set Goals (The Old Way)*, published by Lighthouse Publishing Group, Inc. This book is available in better bookstores.

About The Author

Wade Cook has dedicated his life to teaching and showing people how to retire rich, no matter what their age.

He made his first fortune buying and selling real estate, but not in the traditional way. Like most people, he needed a steady flow of cash, and renting out houses didn't provide it. He discovered that if he fixed up the houses with a minimum amount of cash he could sell them very quickly, sometimes even before his own purchase was completed. The key was that he carried the notes, taking monthly payments from the buyers-instant cash flow! Wade's system became known as the ***Real Estate Money Machine***, thus the title of his first bestselling book.

During the last four years, he has committed himself to intense investment research, development, and practice, creating the most astonishing wealth-building process ever. Initially, Wade intended to use these incredible investment formulas solely to build an even greater wealth for himself and his company. Then, while speaking at a seminar in California, he mentioned that his investment team (Team Wall Street) was earning greater than 300%, often several thousand percent per annum. Needless to say, there was an overwhelming interest expressed by those in attendance prompting Wade to share it with people across the country, like you.

Wade teaches new ways of thinking, ways to change lives and replace failed perceptions. Rather than supplying temporary "Band-

Aids," he gives real life solutions garnered from years of testing and proving various wealth enhancement and cash flow strategies.

Several books, and most important, thousands of successful students later, Wade Cook's Wall Street Workshop has become the premiere stock market course for those interested in creating their own financial independance.

Wade and his family reside on a 40 acre horse ranch in beautiful Washington State—God's country, if you ask him!

Available Resources

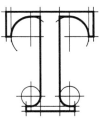

The following books, videos, and audiocassettes have been reviewed by the Wade Cook Seminars, Inc. or Lighthouse Publishing Group, Inc. staff and are suggested as reading and resource material for continuing education to help with your financial planning, and real estate and stock market investments. Because new ideas and techniques come along and laws change, we're always updating our catalogue.

To order a copy of our current catalogue, please write or call us at:

Wade Cook Seminars, Inc.
14675 Interurban Avenue South
Seattle, Washington 98168-4664
1-800-872-7411

Or, visit us on our web sites at:
www.wadecook.com
www.lighthousebooks.com

Also, we would love to hear your comments on our products and services, as well as your testimonials on how these products have benefited you. We look forward to hearing from you!

Audiocassettes

Income Formulas-A free cassette
By Wade B. Cook

Learn the 11 cash flow formulas taught in the Wall Street Workshop. Learn to double some of your money in $2^1/2$ to 4 months.

Zero To Zillions
By Wade B. Cook

This is a powerful audio workshop on Wall Street-understanding the stock market game, playing it successfully, and retiring rich. Learn 11 powerful investment strategies to avoid pitfalls and losses, catch "Day-trippers," "Bottom fish," write Covered Calls, double your money in one week on options on stock split companies, and so much more. Wade "Meter Drop" Cook will teach you how he makes fantastic annual returns in your account.

Power Of Nevada Corporations-A free cassette
By Wade B. Cook

Nevada Corporations have secrecy, privacy, minimal taxes, no reciprocity with the IRS, and protection for shareholders, officers, and directors. This is a powerful seminar.

Income Streams-A free cassette
By Wade B. Cook

Learn to buy and sell real estate the Wade Cook way. This informative cassette will instruct you in building and operating your own real estate money machine.

Money Machine I & II
By Wade B. Cook

Learn the benefits of buying, and more importantly, selling real estate. Now the system for creating and maintaining a real estate money machine is available in audiocassette form. Money Machine I & II teach the step by step cash flow formulas that made Wade Cook and thousands like him millions of dollars.

Money Mysteries of the Millionaires-A free cassette
By Wade B. Cook

How to make money and keep it. This fantastic seminar shows you how to use Nevada Corporations, Living Trusts, Pension Plans, Charitable Remainder Trusts, and Family Limited Partnerships to protect your assets.

Unlimited Wealth Audio Set
By Wade B. Cook

Unlimited Wealth is the "University of Money-Making Ideas" home study course that helps you improve your money's personality. The heart and soul of this seminar is to make more money, pay fewer taxes, and keep more for your retirement and family. This cassette series contains the great ideas from **Wealth 101** on tape, so you can listen to them whenever you want.

Retirement Prosperity
By Wade B. Cook

Take that IRA money now sitting idle and invest it in ways that generate you bigger, better, and quicker returns. This four audiotape set walks you through a system of using a self directed IRA to create phenomenal profits, virtually tax free! This is one of the most complete systems for IRA investing ever created.

The Financial Fortress Home Study Course
By Wade B. Cook

This eight-part series is the last word in entity structuring. It goes far beyond mere financial planning or estate planning. It helps you structure your business and your affairs so that you can avoid the majority of taxes, retire rich, escape lawsuits, bequeath your assets to your heirs without government interference, and, in short-bomb proof your entire estate. There are six audio cassette seminars on tape, an entity structuring video, and a full kit of documents.

Paper Tigers and Paper Chase
By Wade B. Cook

Wade gives you a personal introduction to the art of buying and selling real estate. In this set of six cassettes, Wade shares his inside secrets to establishing a cash flow business with real estate investments. You will learn how to find discounted second mortgages, find second mortgage notes and make them better, as well as how you can get 40%-plus yields on your money. Learn the art of structuring your business to attract investors and bring in the income you desire through the use of family corporations, pension plans, and other legal entities. A manual is included.

When you buy Paper Tigers, you'll also receive Paper Chase for free. Paper Chase holds the most important tools you need to make deals happen. Wade created these powerful tapes as a handout tool you can lend to potential investors or home owners to help educate them about how this amazing cash flow system works for them. It explains how you'll negotiate a lower interest rate if they make a larger payment. You will use this incredible tool over and over again.

High Performance Business Strategies
By Wade B. Cook

Your business cannot succeed without you. This course will help you become successful so your company can succeed. It is a combination of two previous courses, formerly entitled Turbo-Charge Your Business and High-Octane Business Strategies. For years, Wade Cook and his staff have listened to people's questions, and concerns. Because they know that problems are best solved by people who already know the ropes, Wade's staff wanted to help. They categorized the questions and came up with about 60 major areas of concern. Wade then went into the recording studio and dealt head on with these questions. What resulted is a comprehensive collection of knowledge to get you started quickly.

Books

Wall Street Money Machine
By Wade B. Cook

Appearing on the *New York Times* Business Best Sellers list for over one year, **Wall Street Money Machine** contains the best strategies for wealth enhancement and cash flow creation you'll find anywhere. Throughout this book, Wade Cook describes many of his favorite strategies for generating cash flow through the stock market: Rolling Stock, Proxy Investing, Covered Calls, and many more. It's a great introduction for creating wealth using the Wade Cook formulas.

Stock Market Miracles
By Wade B. Cook

The anxiously-awaited partner to **Wall Street Money Machine**, this book is proven to be just as invaluable. **Stock Market Miracles** improves on some of the strategies from **Wall Street Money Machine**, as well as introducing new and valuable twists on our old favorites. This is a must read for anyone interested in making serious money in the stock market.

Bear Market Baloney
By Wade B. Cook

A more timely book wouldn't be possible. Wade's predictions came true while the book was at press! Don't miss this insightful look into what makes bull and bear markets and how to make exponential returns in any market.

Real Estate Money Machine
By Wade B. Cook

Wade's first bestselling book reveals the secrets of Wade Cook's own system-the system he earned his first million from. This book teaches you how to make money regardless of the state of the economy. Wade's innovative concepts for investing in real estate not only avoids high interest rates, but avoids banks altogether.

How To Pick Up Foreclosures
By Wade B. Cook

Do you want to become an expert money maker in real estate? This book will show you how to buy real estate at 60¢ on the dollar or less. You'll learn to find the house before the auction and purchase it with no bank financing-the easy way to millions in real estate. The market for foreclosures is a tremendous place to learn and prosper. *How To Pick Up Foreclosures* takes Wade's methods from *Real Estate Money Machine* and super charges them by applying the fantastic principles to already-discounted properties.

Owner Financing
By Wade B. Cook

This is a short but invaluable booklet you can give to sellers who hesitate to sell you their property using the owner financing method. Let this pamphlet convince both you and them. The special report, *"Why Sellers Should Take Monthly Payments,"* is included for free!

Real Estate For Real People
By Wade B. Cook

A priceless, comprehensive overview of real estate investing, this book teaches you how to buy the right property for the right price, at the right time. Wade Cook explains all of the strategies you'll need, and gives you 20 reasons why you should start investing in real estate today. Learn how to retire rich with real estate, and have fun doing it.

In With A Dime Out With A Dollar
By Wade B. Cook

Wade Cook has personally achieved success after success in real estate. *In With A Dime Out With A Dollar*, formerly 101 Ways To Buy Real Estate Without Cash fills the gap left by other authors who have given all the ingredients but not the whole recipe for real estate investing. This is the book for the investor who wants innovative and practical methods for buying real estate with little or no money down.

Brilliant Deductions
By Wade B. Cook

Do you want to make the most of the money you earn? Do you want to have solid tax havens and ways to reduce the taxes you pay? This book is for you! Learn how to get rich in spite of the updated 1997 tax laws. See new tax credits, year-end maneuvers, and methods for transferring and controlling your entities. Learn to structure yourself and your family for tax savings and liability protection. Available in bookstores or call our toll free number: 1-800-872-7411.

Wealth 101
By Wade B. Cook

This incredible book brings you 101 strategies for wealth creation and protection that you can't afford to miss. Front to back, it is packed full of tips and tricks to supercharge your financial health. If you need to generate more cash flow, this book shows you how through several various avenues. If you are already wealthy, this is the book that will show you strategy upon strategy for decreasing your tax liability and increasing your peace of mind through liability protection.

Videos

Dynamic Dollars Video
By Wade B. Cook

Wade Cook's 90 minute introduction to the basics of his Wall Street formulas and strategies. In this presentation designed especially for video, Wade explains the meter drop philosophy, Rolling Stock, basics of Proxy Investing, and writing Covered Calls. Perfect for anyone looking for a little basic information.

The Wall Street Workshop Video Series
By Wade B. Cook

If you can't make it to the Wall Street Workshop soon, get a head start with these videos. Ten albums containing 11 hours of intense instruction on Rolling Stock, options on stock split companies, writing Covered Calls, and eight other tested and proven strategies designed to help you increase the value of your investments. By learning, reviewing, and implementing the strategies taught here, you will gain the knowledge and the confidence to take control of your investments, and get your money to work hard for you.

The Next Step Video Series
By Team Wall Street

The advanced version of the Wall Street Workshop. Full of power-packed strategies from Wade Cook, this is not a duplicate of the Wall Street Workshop, but a very important partner. The methods taught in this seminar will supercharge the strategies taught in the Wall Street Workshop and teach you even more ways to make more money!

In the Next Step, you'll learn how to find the stocks to fit the formulas through technical analysis, fundamentals, home trading tools, and more.

Build Perpetual Income (BPI)-A videocassette

Wade Cook Seminars, Inc. is proud to present **Build Perpetual Income**, the latest in our ever-expanding series of seminar home study courses. In this video, you will learn powerful real estate cash-flow generating techniques, such as:

- Power negotiating strategies
- Buying and selling mortgages
- Writing contracts
- Finding and buying discount properties
- Avoiding debt

Classes Offered

Cook University

People enroll in **Cook University** for a variety of reasons. Usually they are a little discontented with where they are-their job is not working, their business is not producing the kind of income they want, or they definitely see that they need more income to prepare for a better retirement. That's where **Cook University** comes in. As you try to live the American Dream, in the life-style you want, we stand by ready to assist you make the dream your reality.

The backbone of the one-year program is the Money Machine concept-as applied to your business, to stock investments, or to real estate. Although there are many, many other forms of investing in real estate, there are really only three that work: the Money Machine method, buying second mortgages, and lease options. Of these three, the Money Machine stands head and shoulders above the rest.

It is difficult to explain **Cook University** in only a few words. It is so unique, innovative and creative that it literally stands alone. But then, what would you expect from Wade Cook? Something common and ordinary? Never! Wade and his staff always go out of their way to provide you with useful, tried-and-true strategies that create real wealth.

We are embarking on an unprecedented voyage and want you to come along. If you choose to make this important decision in your life, you could also be invited to share your successes in a series of books called *Blueprints For Success* (more volumes to come). Yes, it takes commitment. Yes, it takes drive. Add to this the help you'll receive by our hand-trained experts and you will enhance your asset base and increase your bottom line.

We want to encourage a lot of people to get in the program right away. You could save thousands of dollars, if you don't delay. Call right away! Class sizes are limited so each student gets personal attention.

Perpetual monthly income is waiting. We'll teach you how to achieve it. We'll show you how to make it. We'll watch over you while you're making it happen. Thank you for your consideration. We hope to see you in the program right away.

Cook University is designed to be an integral part of your educational life. We encourage you to call and find out more about this life-changing program. The number is 1-800-872-7411. Ask for an enrollment director and begin your millionaire-training today!

If you want to be wealthy, this is the place to be.

The Wall Street Workshop
Presented by Wade B. Cook and Team Wall Street
The Wall Street Workshop teaches you how to make incredible money in all markets. It teaches you the tried-and-true strategies that have made hundreds of people wealthy.

The Next Step Workshop
Presented by Wade B. Cook and Team Wall Street
An Advanced Wall Street Workshop designed to help those ready to take their trading to the next level and treat it as a business. This seminar is open only to graduates of the Wall Street Workshop.

Executive Retreat
Presented by Wade B. Cook and Team Wall Street
Created especially for the individuals already owning or planning to establish Nevada Corporations, the Executive Retreat is a unique opportunity for corporate executives to participate in workshops geared toward streamlining operations and maximizing efficiency and impact.

Wealth Academy
Presented by Wade B. Cook and Team Wall Street

This three day workshop defines the art of asset protection and entity planning. During these three days we will discuss, in depth and detail, the six domestic entities which will protect you from lawsuits, taxes, or other financial losses, and help you retire rich.

Real Estate Workshop
Presented by Wade B. Cook and Team Main Street

The Real Estate Workshop teaches you how to build perpetual income for life, without going to work. Some of the topics include buying and selling paper, finding discounted properties, generating long-term monthly cash flow, and controlling properties wihtout owning them.

Real Estate Bootcamp
Presented by Wade B. Cook and Team Main Street

This three to four day Bootcamp is truly a roll-up-your-sleeves-and-do-the-deals event. You will be learning how to locate the bargains, negotiate strategies, and find wholesale properties (pre-foreclosures). You will also visit a title company, look at properties and learn some new and fun selling strategies.

Business Entity Skills Training (BEST)
Presented by Wade B. Cook and Team Wall Street

Learn about the six powerful entities you can use to protect your wealth and your family. Learn the secrets of asset protection, eliminate your fear of litigation, and minimize your taxes.

Assorted Resources

Wealth Information Network (WIN)

This subscription computer bulletin board service provides you with the latest financial formulas and updated entity structuring strategies. New, timely information is entered Monday through Friday, sometimes four or five times a day. Wade Cook and his Team Wall Street staff write for **WIN**, giving you updates on their own current stock plays, companies who announced earnings, companies who announced stock splits, and the latest trends in the market.

WIN is also divided into categories according to specific strategies and contains archives of all our trades so you can view our history. If you are just getting started in the stock market, this is a great way to follow people who are doubling their money every $2^1/2$ to 4 months. If you are experienced already, it's the way to confirm your feelings and research with others who are generating wealth through the stock market.

IQ Pager

This is a system which beeps you as events and announcements are made on Wall Street. With **IQ Pager**, you'll receive information about events like major stock split announcements, earnings surprises, important mergers and acquisitions, judgements or court decisions involving big companies, important bankruptcy announcements, big winners and losers, and disasters. If you're getting your financial information from the evening news, you're getting it too late. The key to the stock market is timing. Especially when you're trading in options, you need up-to-the-minute (or second) information. You cannot afford to sit at a computer all day looking for news or wait for your broker to call. **IQ Pager** is the ideal partner to the Wealth Information Network (WIN).

The Incorporation Handbook
By Wade B. Cook

Incorporation made easy! This handbook tells you who, why, and, most importantly, how to incorporate. Included are samples of the forms you will use when you incorporate, as well as a step-by-step guide from the experts.

Legal Forms
By Wade B. Cook

This collection of pertinent forms contains numerous legal forms used in real estate transactions. These forms were selected by experienced investors, but are not intended to replace the advice of an attorney. However, they will provide essential forms for you to follow in your personal investing.

Record Keeping System
By Wade B. Cook

A complete record keeping system for organizing all of the information on each of your properties. This system keeps track of everything from insurance policies to equity growth. You will know at a glance exactly where you stand with your investment properties and you will sleep better at night.

Travel Agent Information
By John Childers and Wade Cook

The only sensible solution for the frequent traveller. This kit includes all of the information and training you need to be an outside travel agent for a stable company. There are no hassles, no requirements, no forms or restrictions, just all the benefits of travelling for substantially less every time.

DATE